ASIA

Pacific Ocean

E

AFRICA

Indian Ocean

AUSTRALASIA

Photo Credits
All Sport (UK) Ltd; Amey Roadstone Corporation; Heather Angel; Apple and Pear Development Council; Ardea; Nick Birch; Paul Brierley; Pat Brindley; BBC; British Airways; British Museum; British Telecom; British Airways Board; British Tourist Authority; Bruker Meerestechnik GMBH; Carl Byoir Association; Canon (UK) Ltd; J. Allan Cash; Michael Chinery; Philip Clarke; Bruce Coleman Ltd; The Dance Library; Douglas Dickins; Esso; French Government Tourist Office; Frank Gibberd Coombes and Partners; Stanley Gibbons; Ken Gilham; Steve Godfrey; Hale Observatory; Michael Holford; The Hutchison Library; Japanese Information Centre; Kenya Coffee Board; Geoffrey Kinns; Lick Observatory; W.M. Macquitty; Dr R. Maddison; Stella Martin; May and Baker; Metropolitan Museum of Art; Millbrook House Limited/C.M. Whitehouse; Montana Chamber of Commerce; Pat Morris; NASA; NASA/Mat Irvine; National Gallery; National Maritime Museum; National Portrait Gallery; National Trust Photographic Library; Natural History Picture Agency; Natural Science Photos; New Holland Ltd; Novosti; Peabody Museum; Photri; Picturepoint; Royal National Lifeboat Institution; Shell; Science Museum; Space Frontiers; Spectrum; Frank Spooner Pictures; Swiss National Tourist Office; Syndication International; Tate Gallery; Tea Council; TIMEX Corporation Ltd; Trans-Globe; Robert Updegraff; Walker Art Gallery; Peter Newark's Western Americana; Janine Wiedel; Reg Wilson; John Youé; ZEFA.

First published 1988
Reprinted 1989

Published by
MACMILLAN CHILDREN'S BOOKS
A division of Macmillan Publishers
4 Little Essex Street, London WC2R 3LF
and Basingstoke
Companies and representatives
throughout the world

Printed in Hong Kong

Turner, Dorothy
   The Macmillan first encyclopedia
   1. Children's encyclopedias and dictionaries
   I. Title
   032   AG5

ISBN 0-333-44259-8

The Macmillan First Encyclopedia

M

Macmillan Children's Books

A Actor Africa

Actor

Films and plays tell stories. Actors pretend to be the people in the stories. They try to be as much like the story people as they can. They wear special costumes and make-up to help them do this. They learn all the words that the people in the story are saying.

These children are acting in a play.

Africa

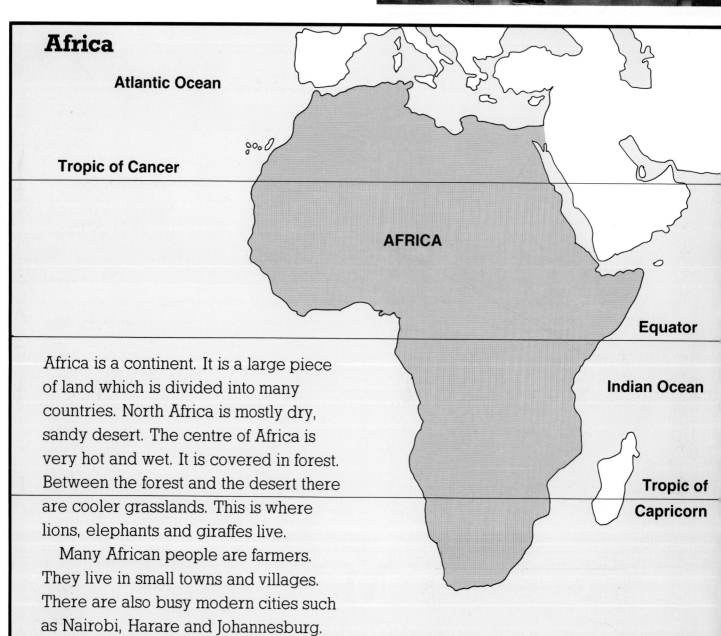

Atlantic Ocean

Tropic of Cancer

AFRICA

Equator

Indian Ocean

Tropic of Capricorn

Africa is a continent. It is a large piece of land which is divided into many countries. North Africa is mostly dry, sandy desert. The centre of Africa is very hot and wet. It is covered in forest. Between the forest and the desert there are cooler grasslands. This is where lions, elephants and giraffes live.

Many African people are farmers. They live in small towns and villages. There are also busy modern cities such as Nairobi, Harare and Johannesburg.

Amphibians

Animals that can live in water and on land are called amphibians. These animals lay their eggs in the water. Their young swim and breathe through gills like fish. Fully grown amphibians have legs. They breathe through lungs. Frogs and toads are amphibians.

Ancient Greeks

More than 4000 years ago people came to live in south-eastern Europe. We call that land Greece. The people made their homes in towns and villages. They built beautiful cities, like Athens and Sparta. Each city made its own laws.

The people made fine statues and pottery and jewellery. They liked music and plays and all kinds of sports. Greek doctors, thinkers and mathematicians were among the best in the world. Greek people worshipped many gods and goddesses.

Below: Helios, the sun god, and his chariot.

Animals

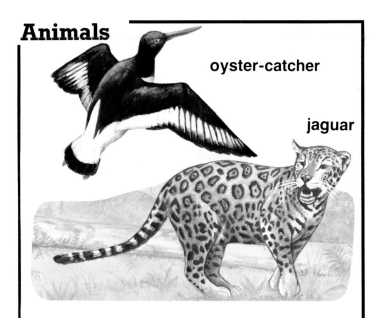

oyster-catcher

jaguar

Birds, mammals, reptiles, fish and insects are all animals. Human beings are mammals, so we are animals too.

There are more than two million different kinds of animals. Some are cold-blooded. Others are warm-blooded. Some are so small that they can only be seen with a microscope. Others, like the blue whale, are huge. Animals live even in the hottest and the coldest places on Earth.

scarlet snake

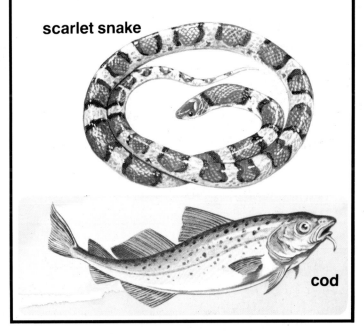

cod

A Ant Antarctica Apple

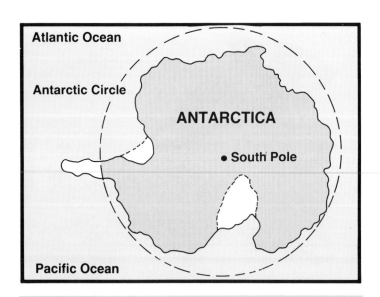

Antarctica

Antarctica is an enormous piece of icy land around the South Pole. It is the coldest place on Earth. Scientists go there to study it, but it is too cold for people to stay for long. There are no land animals, except for a few tiny insects. There are a few plants, but no trees. Only penguins, seals and sea birds live there.

Apple

Apples are a kind of fruit. The pips inside are seeds which grow into apple trees. Millions of apples are grown each year for us to eat. Some of them are made into a drink called cider.

Ant

Above: An ant carrying a flower to its nest.

Ants are small insects. They live in huge groups called colonies. Some ants build underground tunnels and live there. Others build tall ant hills.

There is a queen ant in every colony. She lays eggs. Male ants mate with her so that more eggs can be laid. The other females are worker ants. They build the nest, collect food and look after the young ants. This worker ant is taking food to the nest.

Below: A man loading a bin with apples.

Above: An archaeologist looking for remains of the past.

Archaeologist

Archaeologists are interested in how people lived long ago. They look for things like coins, pottery and the remains of buildings. Things that people who lived long ago made will tell how they lived. Sometimes archaeologists have to dig in the ground to find things.

Architect

Architects design buildings. They make drawings showing all the parts of a building. The plans show the builder exactly how to make the building.

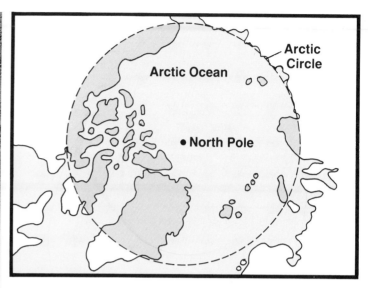

Arctic

The Arctic is the area around the North Pole. Most of it is frozen sea. The long Arctic winter is very cold and dark. In the short summer the sun shines all the time, even at night. Flowers, moss and small bushes grow in the summer.

The Inuit and Saami peoples live in the Arctic. Reindeer, seals and polar bears also live there.

A Armed forces

Armed forces

US Army

Australian Navy

Royal Air Force

The army, navy and air force are called the armed forces. They protect a country from attack. The army protects on land. The navy protects at sea. The air force protects in the air. Soldiers, sailors and airmen and women wear clothes called uniforms.

Army

The soldier in the top picture is a member of the US Army. Modern armies use tanks, guns and missiles. The army is the oldest part of the armed forces. There have been armies for thousands of years.

Navy

The sailor on the left is wearing the uniform of the Australian Navy. Navies use powerful ships and submarines. Some ships carry fighter planes. They are called aircraft carriers. The planes take off from the deck of the aircraft carrier.

Air Force

This British airman is a member of the Royal Air Force. The picture shows a Tornado, a jet fighter plane. Modern air forces use fighters like these. They travel twice as fast as sound.

Armour

Soldiers wore armour to protect their bodies in battle. Armour was made of leather and metal. Foot soldiers wore light armour. Soldiers on horseback wore very heavy armour. If they fell they could not get up without help.

Today the police sometimes wear helmets and carry shields. This is called riot gear.

Astronaut

Astronauts are people who travel into space in space ships. The word means 'star sailor'. They take their food, water and air supply with them. They wear special suits.

Yuri Gagarin made the first space flight in 1961. Since then, many men and women have travelled in space. People can now walk in space too.

Above: The astronaut Bruce McCandless in space.

Left: Battle armour.

Astronomer

An astronomer studies all the planets and stars in the universe. The first astronomers lived thousands of years ago. They had no equipment to help them. They could study only what they could see with their eyes. When telescopes were invented astronomers were able to see much more of the sky.

Telescopes make objects in space look clearer and closer. Modern astronomers use enormous telescopes like the one in the picture.

Today, some astronomers use radio telescopes. They do not look through these telescopes. Instead, they listen to the sounds that the telescopes pick up from space. These sounds tell astronomers what is happening very far away in space.

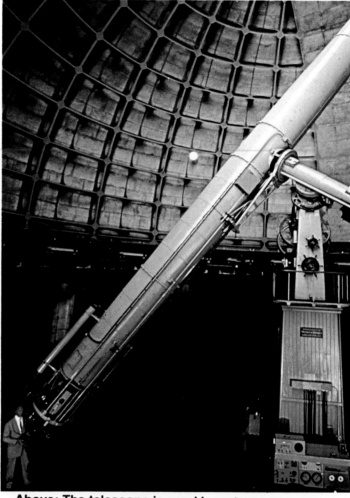

Above: The telescope is used by astronomers to see distant stars and planets.

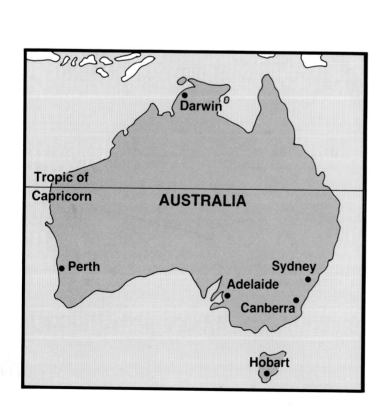

Australia

Australia is a huge island. Much of it is hot dry desert. Australian sheep farmers produce more than a quarter of the world's wool. Most people live on the south east coast where there is more rain. They live in big modern cities. The capital city is near the east coast. It is called Canberra.

Kangaroos and koala bears are Australian animals. They carry their young in pouches. These animals are found nowhere else in the world.

Bach (1685-1750)

Johann Sebastian Bach was born in Germany. He wrote fine music full of complicated patterns of sound. Bach was a very religious man. He worked as a church organist and choir master for most of his life. Many of his famous pieces of music were written to be played on the organ. Bach also wrote religious music for choirs to sing in church.

Balloon

Above: A modern gas balloon about to take off.

This balloon is filled with gas. It rises up into the air. So do party balloons and balloons filled with hot air. Hot air balloons were used by people long before planes were invented. The people sat in a basket which was fastened underneath.

Bank

Banks look after people's money for them. If you want to use your money to buy things you have a current account and a cheque book. You write cheques instead of giving people coins and notes (cash).

If you are going abroad you can exchange your money for foreign money at a bank. You can also keep jewellery or other valuable things at the bank.

Bat

Bats are flying mammals. They fly by using their arms and a wing of skin. Most bats come out in the evening.

Bats catch their prey in the air. They do this by making squeaking sounds. The sounds bounce back and tell the bat if there is anything in its way. Most bats eat insects and small animals. They usually sleep through the winter in caves or in dark corners of buildings or barns.

B Bear Beaver Bee

Bear

Bears are large, strong, meat-eating animals. There are several different kinds of bears and they have thick, furry coats. This brown bear lives in North America. Black bears and grizzlies live there too. They eat berries, insects, honey and meat. Polar bears are large bears which live in the Arctic. Alaskan Kodiac bears are the largest bears.

Beaver

Beavers are rodents. All rodents have long front teeth for gnawing. Beavers always live near water, and they are very good swimmers. Sometimes they gnaw down small trees and pull them across a stream. A pond forms behind the trees. Then the beavers build a home safe in the middle of the pond.

Bee

Bees are flying insects. They live in large groups. Honey bees often nest in boxes called hives. Every group of bees has a queen. She lays eggs. The other female bees are workers. They look after the queen and the young bees. They collect nectar from flowers and take it back to the hive. There, it is made into honey. Male bees are called drones. They do not work in the hive. It is their job to mate with the queen bee so that more eggs can be laid.

Beethoven Beetle Bird Bread B

Beethoven (1770-1827)

Ludwig van Beethoven was a composer and a musician. He was born in Germany. When he was a child he was a brilliant musician. Later, Beethoven wrote music for orchestras to play. He also wrote music especially for the piano and violin, and songs too. When he was about 30, Beethoven became deaf. He could not hear his music, but he continued to write.

Beetle

Beetles are insects. They have two pairs of wings. The back wings are used for flying. The front wings fold over to make the beetle's hard shiny cover. Beetle eggs hatch into grubs. The grubs change into chrysalides. Then the beetles hatch out of the chrysalides. There are many kinds of beetle. Ladybirds are beetles. The stag beetles in the picture are fighting each other.

Bird

Birds are warm-blooded animals that lay eggs. They are covered in feathers, and almost all birds can fly.

There are birds all over the world. Some eat meat or fish. Others eat insects, seeds or fruit. Many birds fly to warmer places in the winter.

Below: Two male stag beetles fighting.

Bread

People discovered how to make bread thousands of years ago. It was one of the first foods they made.

All bread is made from flour. Flour is made when grains of wheat or rye are ground very finely. Yeast is added to the flour and water. It makes the bread rise. Bread baked with yeast is light and airy. In parts of Africa, India and the Middle East, they make flat or unleavened bread. It does not contain yeast so it is dense and heavy.

B Buddha Butterfly

Buddha

A statue of the Great Buddha at Kamakura in Japan.

The man called 'the Buddha' was born in India about 2500 years ago. His name was Siddhartha Gautama and his family was very rich. Gautama wanted to find out why people were unhappy. So he left his family and his rich life. He travelled around, living a simple life without much money. Gautama began to teach people how to live. People called him 'the Buddha'. It means a person with special knowledge. The Buddha did not believe in a god. He thought people should live good lives. No one should harm another person or living thing. People who follow his teaching today live a simple life, as he did.

Butterfly

Butterflies are flying insects with brightly coloured wings. They feed on nectar from flowers. They suck the nectar up through their long, hollow tongues. Most butterflies live for only a short time.

Butterflies lay eggs on leaves. The eggs hatch into caterpillars. Most caterpillars eat leaves. When they have eaten enough, they spin a thread or pad. They stick to a twig. Their skin hardens and they turn into a chrysalis. Inside the chrysalis the caterpillar slowly changes into a butterfly.

The butterfly breaks out of the chrysalis and flies away.

caterpillar

egg

chrysalis

adult

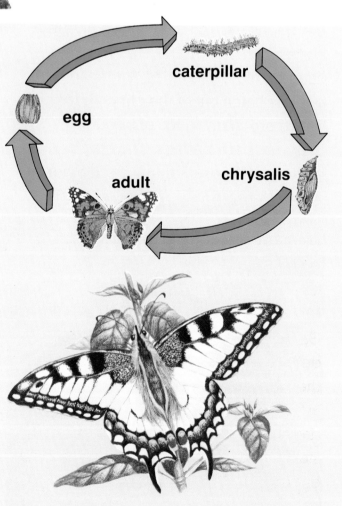

Cactus

Cacti are plants which grow in hot, dry places. They have special thick stems which can store water. This helps them to live in the desert where there is very little rain. Many cacti have beautiful bright flowers. There are many different shapes of cactus. Some of them are round and prickly. Others are thin and grow as tall as trees.

Camel

Camels are used to carry loads in the desert. Their broad feet help to spread their weight over soft sand. Camels store water in their bodies. They can go for days and weeks without drinking. They store fat in their humps. This gives them energy when there is not much food to eat.

Camera

Cameras take photographs. At the front of the camera there is a small glass window. It is called a lens. Behind the lens there is a shutter. When you press a button on the camera the shutter opens. Light goes in through the lens. It makes a picture on the film inside the camera. Then the shutter closes.

The picture stays on the film. When the film is printed we can see the picture. It is a photograph.

C Camouflage Canal Captain Cook

Camouflage

Some animals look like their surroundings. This is called camouflage. Camouflage protects an animal or helps it to hunt.

This insect looks like the green leaf. The fish looks like the pebbles in the stream. The spots make the cheetah hard to see in the long grass.

Canal

Canals are waterways built by people. First the canal is dug out of the land and then it is flooded with water. Some canals are quite shallow. Flat-bottomed boats called barges sail on them. Other canals are deep and wide enough to let large tankers sail through them.

Below: The Corinth Canal, Greece.

Captain Cook (1728-1779)

Captain James Cook was a famous British explorer. He lived about 200 years ago. He sailed all over the Pacific Ocean. People knew very little about this ocean until he sailed there.

Cook sailed to Australia and New Zealand. He also visited many small Pacific islands. He studied the plants, animals and peoples of these islands. Cook made careful maps of the places he visited.

Car

Cars are very complicated machines. They are made of thousands of parts. Most cars need petrol to make the engines work. Some cars use diesel fuel. A few cars are electric. The engine drives the wheels. When the wheels turn, the car moves along the road.

Castle

Castles were built to protect people from attack. They had strong, thick walls. Some had a ditch of water, called a moat, all round the outside. Many castles were built on hills. The soldiers inside could fire arrows and throw stones down on their enemies.

The lord and lady and their family, servants and soldiers lived in the castle. Each castle had a big hall and a kitchen. There were many smaller rooms where people could sleep. Also, there were rooms where food was stored and places where weapons were kept.

Cat

Pet cats, lions, tigers and leopards all belong to the cat family. There are many different kinds of pet cats. In the picture are a tabby cat and a Siamese cat. The Siamese cat has bright blue eyes.

Cats hunt at night. Pet cats, like lions, creep up quietly on their prey. Then they spring out and catch their prey with their claws.

tabby cat

Siamese cat

C Cave Cave people Cereals

Cave

A cave is a hollow place in the rocks. Most caves are found in limestone rocks. Rainwater slowly dissolves the limestone. After many years, caves and tunnels are left where the rain has been. Sometimes, columns of limestone grow down from the cave roof. These are called stalactites. Stalagmites grow from the cave floor.

Cave people

In earliest times, some people lived in caves. Caves protected them from wild animals and the cold weather. They knew how to make fire and they made stone tools. They ate berries and fruit and they made their clothes from animal skins.

Cereals

Cereals are important plants because they give us food. Wheat, rice, oats, barley and maize are cereals. They all belong to the grass family.

Farmers plant cereal crops in their fields. When the plants are fully grown they are cut down. Many cereals provide food for animals. Some, like wheat, are made into flour. The heads of the wheat are ground up to make the flour. Some cereal crops are used to make our breakfast foods.

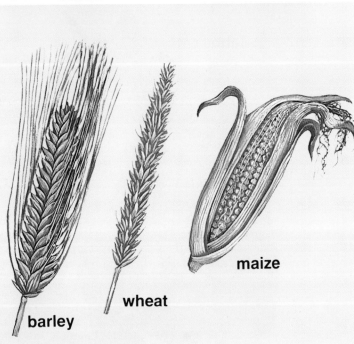

barley

wheat

maize

Cheetah

The cheetah is a member of the cat family. Cheetahs have very long legs. They are the fastest land animals. They can run at up to 112 kilometres per hour. In India people used to train cheetahs to hunt other animals. Now there are not many cheetahs left in India. Most cheetahs live in Africa. Cheetahs hunt in pairs at sunrise and sunset when it is cooler.

Chimpanzee

The chimpanzee is a kind of ape. It lives in the African rainforests. Groups of chimpanzees travel together through the forests. They look for fruit and plant shoots to eat. They also eat birds' eggs and small animals. At night they rest in trees. Chimpanzees are very intelligent. They can use tools, such as sticks, to help them find food.

China

Life in China is changing. Until about 70 years ago China was ruled by royal families. Most people were poor farmers. They worked for rich landlords. Now people farm the land together. The farms are called communes. They grow cotton, rice, fruit and vegetables.

China is an industrial country too. There are new factories, roads and power stations.

Five million people live in the capital city, Beijing.

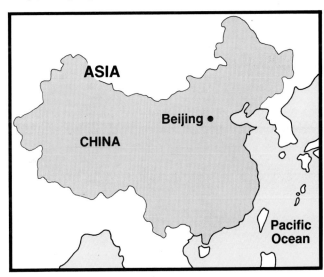

C Christmas Church Circus

Christmas

Christmas is the time of year when Christians remember the birth of Jesus Christ. There are special services in church. Everyone has a holiday.

It is also a time to think about other people. People give each other presents. They send cards to their friends and meet to have parties.

Church

Churches are buildings where Christians worship God. Christians follow the teachings of Jesus Christ. Their holy book, the Bible, tells them about Jesus. They try to live in the way that Jesus taught.

There are special times when people go to church. Babies are christened there. People get married there. When people die, a funeral service is held for them in the church.

Circus

At a circus you can see people and animals doing clever tricks. Some people walk on high wires or swing through the air on trapezes. Others turn somersaults or juggle. Clowns paint their faces and make people laugh.

Circus families live in caravans and travel from place to place. Their children often learn how to be circus performers too.

Below: Tight-rope walkers in a circus.

Below: A parish church.

Clock

Above: An analogue clock.

A clock tells us the time. The wheels and springs inside it turn the hands. The hands point to numbers on the clock face. We wind clocks up to keep them going.

Blind people have special clocks and watches. There are raised dots on the clock face. They cannot see the time, but they can feel it.

Digital clocks do not have wheels and springs. Numbers light up to show the time. They are worked by electricity. Digital clocks and watches have tiny batteries inside.

Below: A digital clock.

Coal

Above: Miners working in a coal mine.

Coal was made from plants that lived on Earth millions of years ago. The plants died and were pressed down by rocks. They turned into coal.

Coal is found underground. Miners make long tunnels to reach it. They cut out the coal. Machines help them to do this.

Coal is used to heat houses and to make factories and power stations work.

Cocoa

The cocoa powder used for making drinks and chocolate comes from the seeds of a small tree. This tree is called the cacao tree. The seeds are called beans. They grow inside a pod which is about 15 centimetres long. Both the flowers and the pods hang down from the trunk of the trees. They also hang from the branches. After the cocoa beans have been picked, they are cooked. Then they have to be dried by the heat of the sun before the cocoa can be removed.

Coffee

The coffee we drink is made from beans. The beans come from coffee bushes that grow in hot countries. Fruit grows on these bushes. Inside each fruit there are two beans. People pick the fruit and take out the coffee beans. The beans are roasted and crushed. Coffee is made by pouring hot water on to the crushed beans.

Below: A woman picking coffee beans.

Columbus (1451-1506)

Christopher Columbus was a famous explorer. In 1492 he sailed from Spain and reached the east coast of America. He called the islands there the West Indies.

At that time, most people believed the world was flat. They thought Columbus's ships would fall off the edge of the world. Columbus thought the world was round and he was right.

Combine harvester

Combine harvesters are huge farm machines that harvest crops. They do two jobs at once. The blades at the front cut down a crop, such as corn. Then the machine separates the grains of corn from the stalks. One driver with one combine harvester can cut down large fields of corn very quickly.

Common Market

There are 35 countries in Europe. More than 650 million people live there. Each country has its own language, its own laws and its own way of life.

Some of the countries in western Europe are part of the Common Market. They have agreed about how to grow and sell their farm crops. They also try to agree about where to sell the things each country makes. These are goods such as cars or machine parts.

The Common Market is also called the European Economic Community (EEC).

Compass

A compass shows you which direction you are facing. It is made of a magnetic needle inside a box. The needle swings round, but when it stops it always points north. This drawing shows the points of the compass – north, south, east and west. North points to the North Pole. South points to the South Pole.

Computer

A computer is a machine that stores information. It helps people to work out answers to difficult problems. It does this very quickly. The answers are usually printed out on long sheets of paper. A computer cannot think for itself. People have to give it all the information first. They write programs for the computer, using special language. FORTRAN, ALGOL and BASIC are computer languages.

Computers are used in many places. Offices, shops, banks and factories use them. Hospitals and libraries use them too.

Concorde

Concorde is the first supersonic airliner. This means it can travel faster than the speed of sound.

Concorde can fly from London to New York in three and a half hours. Other airliners take five to seven hours. It carries about 120 passengers. It was planned and made by Britain and France together.

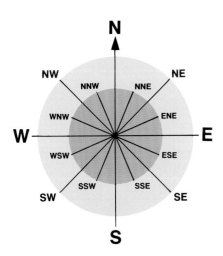

Above: The main compass points: N=North, E=East, S=South and W=West.

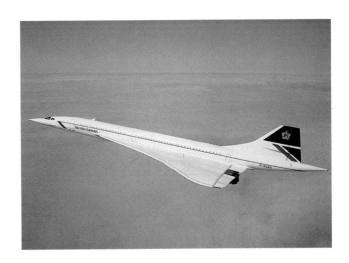

C Cow Crab Crane

Cow

Cows are female cattle. They are very useful animals because they give us milk. There are many different kinds of cow. The cow in the picture is a black and white Friesian.

All cows eat grass. They spend most of the day in the farmer's fields. They chew the grass slowly and carefully. This is called chewing the cud. At the end of the day, the farmer brings the cows to the farm to be milked. Then the milk is taken to dairies. Most of it is put into cartons and bottles. The rest is made into cheese and butter.

Crane

A crane is used to move heavy loads. It lifts the load and swings it round to put it in the right place. The driver of this huge crane sits in the little cabin at the top of the tower.

Crab

The crab lives in the sea. It has a hard shell and five pairs of legs. The front legs are large pincers. The crab uses them to catch food. Crabs walk along the sea bed looking for small creatures to eat. Crabs breathe through gills in the same way as fish. They have eyes on stalks that can be drawn back into their heads. Crabs move by running along sideways. Look for them running on the seashore.

Crocodile

Siamese crocodile

Crocodiles are reptiles. They are cold-blooded animals with dry, scaly skins. They lay their eggs in nests which they build on river banks. Most crocodiles live in warm, tropical rivers. They spend much of the day lying in the sun. Sometimes they float in the water with only the top of their heads and their snouts showing above the surface.

Crocodiles' nostrils are on top of their snouts, so they can breathe when they are floating. They are good swimmers but they cannot walk well on land. Crocodiles eat fish and animals. They have very sharp teeth. Sometimes they attack people who get too close.

Cutty Sark

The Cutty Sark was a famous sailing ship. It had three masts and many sails. It used the strong winds to blow it from one part of the world to another. It was built about 100 years ago to bring tea to England from China.

The crew lived in tiny cabins on the deck. Below deck, the ship was packed full of tea. The Cutty Sark sailed from China to London in 100 days. At the time this was very fast.

A model of the Cutty Sark.

D Dancing Darwin Desert

Above: Ballet dancers.

Dancing

People dance for many different reasons. Cave people danced long ago. They made pictures of their dances on cave walls. People danced to make the rains come to water their crops. They danced before a battle and when they had won it.

Today there are all kinds of dance. Some people like ballroom dancing. Some dance to pop music. Others like to watch special kinds of dancing. Ballet is a dance which tells a story. Each story has its own steps.

Most countries have their own special dances. They are called folk dances.

Darwin (1809-1882)

Charles Darwin was a British scientist. He studied how plants and animals grew and changed slowly over millions of years. They changed so that they had a better chance of staying alive.

Darwin also studied how different kinds of animals are related. He said that human beings are related to apes and monkeys. People were very shocked by Darwin's ideas. Some people thought that God made everything, all at the same time.

Desert

A desert is a place where very little rain falls. Most deserts are very hot. Some are sandy and others are rocky. Only animals and plants that do not need much water can live there. There are large hot deserts in Africa, Australia and North America. Deserts can be very cold at night.

A sandy desert.

Dinghy

A dinghy is a small boat. It can be driven by oars or sails. The wind fills the dinghy's sails and pushes it through the water.

Dinghy sailing is a popular sport. Many people enjoy racing each other in dinghies.

These people are launching their dinghy from a trailer.

Dinosaur

Dinosaurs were reptiles that lived on Earth millions of years ago. There were many different kinds of dinosaurs. Some were enormous. Some were as small as hens. Some dinosaurs were meat-eaters but most ate plants. All of them were cold-blooded and had scaly skins. They all laid eggs.

The fierce meat-eating dinosaurs had sharp teeth like daggers. They ran on their large hind legs and ate other dinosaurs. You can see one of the huge plant-eaters in this picture. They walked slowly on all four legs.

Some plant-eaters were covered in sharp spikes and horny plates. These protected the dinosaurs when they were attacked. Dinosaurs lived long before people. We know about them from fossils. Nobody knows exactly why they all died out.

The Apatosaurus, a plant-eating dinosaur.

D Docks Dodo Dog Dolphin

Docks

Docks are places where ships can be loaded, unloaded or repaired. Huge cranes lift cargo on and off the ships. The cargo is often stored in large warehouses on the dockside.

Special dry docks are made for repairing ships. The ship sails into the dock. Then the water is pumped away. The part of the ship that is usually under water can then be repaired.

Dodo

Dodos were big clumsy birds that could not fly. They lived on an island in the Indian Ocean. They were all killed by people who ate them. Now there are no dodos. They are extinct.

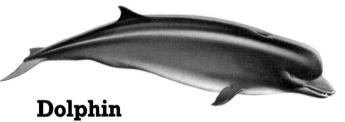

Dolphin

Dolphins are small whales. They are mammals, so they use lungs to breathe air. They live in warm seas and come up to the surface to breathe. They have beaky snouts or noses. Dolphins have many sharp teeth to help them to catch fish. Sometimes they swim near the shore but they are also seen far out at sea. They are very intelligent.

Dog

Dogs are intelligent and useful animals. People have kept tame dogs from the earliest times. Today most dogs are kept as pets or to guard people's homes. Some are used to guard or to move herds of animals. All tame dogs are related to wolves and wild dogs.

Eagle　Earthquake　Eclipse　E

Eagle

Eagles are meat-eating birds. They have strong hooked beaks for tearing meat. Eagles eat small animals and birds. Some sea-eagles eat fish. Eagles fly high in the sky looking down for their prey. They have very good eyesight. They swoop down quickly and catch their prey in their claws. Most eagles live in wild, mountainous places. Their nests are called eyries.

Earthquake

The Earth has an outer layer of rock. Sometimes the rock is cracked. The cracks are called faults. Earthquakes happen when the cracked rocks move. The ground shakes. Buildings fall down. Sometimes people are killed. In some places there are many earthquakes. Houses are built in a special way to stop them falling. In Mexico City about 7000 people died in an earthquake in 1985.

Below: Damage caused by the earthquake in Mexico City in 1985.

Eclipse

An eclipse of the Sun happens when the Moon comes between the Earth and the Sun. The Moon blocks the Sun's light. The part of the Earth facing the Sun becomes as dark as night.

An eclipse of the Moon happens when the Earth comes between the Sun and the Moon. The sunlight cannot reach the Moon. It gives the Earth a shadow. This shadow passes across the Moon.

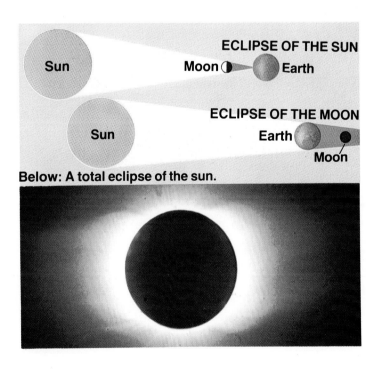

ECLIPSE OF THE SUN

Sun　Moon　Earth

ECLIPSE OF THE MOON

Sun　Earth　Moon

Below: A total eclipse of the sun.

E Eel Egg Electricity Elephant

Eel

Eels are long snake-like fish. There are many different kinds. Common eels live in rivers in Europe. When they are fully grown, they swim out to the middle of the Atlantic Ocean to lay their eggs. The young eels hatch out and swim back to the same rivers. It takes them three years to swim back.

Conger eels are bigger than common eels. They live in the sea all the time.

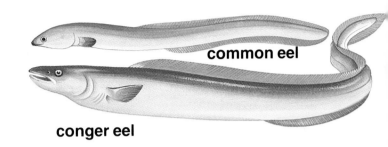

common eel

conger eel

Egg

Female animals produce eggs. When sperm from a male joins with an egg, a young animal begins to grow inside.

Birds and reptiles have eggs with hard shells. The mother lays the eggs in a nest. The young grow inside. The young hatch out when they are grown. This chick has just hatched out.

Fish lay their eggs in the water. Many insects lay their eggs on leaves.

Mammals' eggs grow inside the mother's body. The baby animal stays there until it is ready to be born. This is what happens to human babies.

Electricity

Electricity is an important kind of power. It is made in power stations. The machine that makes it is called a generator. The electricity travels from the power station along wires. Then it reaches our homes, schools and factories. It gives us heat and light. It also makes machines work.

Elephant

Elephants are the largest land animals. African elephants have large ears. The ears of Indian elephants are smaller. All elephants eat fruit and plants, and they drink a lot of water. They suck water up into their trunks and squirt it into their mouths. They also use their trunks to put food into their mouths. Elephants live together in groups called herds.

Elizabeth I (1533-1603)

Queen Elizabeth was one of England's greatest rulers. While she was Queen, England became a richer and more powerful country. There was less fighting than before and explorers set off to discover the world. William Shakespeare and many other famous writers lived during her reign.

Elizabeth liked to look very grand. She had many wigs and fine dresses. She never married, so she had no child to rule after her when she died.

Above: Queen Elizabeth I.

Emerald

Emeralds are precious gems that are transparent and have a bright green colour. Emeralds have to be mined, or dug out of the ground. Most emeralds come from mines in the United States, South America or the Ural Mountains in the USSR. They have to be cut with special tools before they can be made into jewellery.

Below: A pair of emerald and diamond earrings.

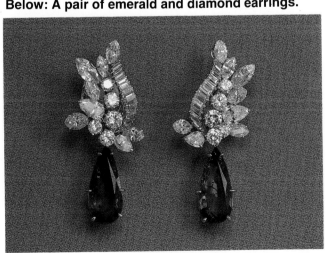

Engineer

There are many different kinds of engineering jobs. Some engineers design new machines. Some use machines to help them build other things. Some repair broken machinery.

New roads and bridges are designed by engineers. Computers and other electrical machines are built by them. They also design engines for cars, trains, ships and planes.

Equator

The Equator is a line drawn on maps of the world. It runs round the middle of the Earth. It is halfway between the North Pole and the South Pole. You can see the Equator on the maps at the beginning and end of this book.

F Fireworks Fish

Fireworks

Fireworks fill the sky with noise and colour. They are used to celebrate special occasions. The bangs are made by gunpowder. The colours are made by chemicals. Rockets fly up into the sky. Burning gases escaping from the rocket force it upwards.

Fish

Fish live in water and breathe through gills. They lay their eggs in the water (picture 1). These eggs hatch into larvae (picture 2). Fully grown fish have tails and fins which help them to swim in the water (picture 3).

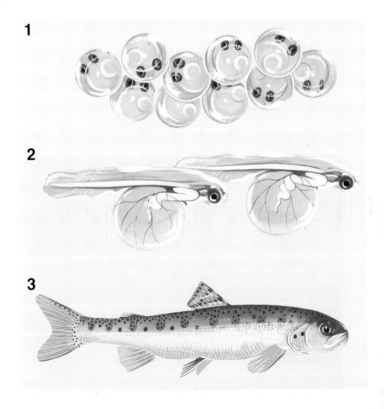

flowers

Flowers make seeds. New plants can grow from these seeds. Many flowers, like the rose and the orchid, are very beautiful and have a sweet smell. The colour and scent attract insects to the flower. Other plants, like the nettle, have small flowers. Each dandelion flower head is made of hundreds of small flowers called florets which grow together. Waterlilies float on ponds. The Venus fly-trap has tiny flowers. It traps insects in its large, spiked leaves. Then it digests them.

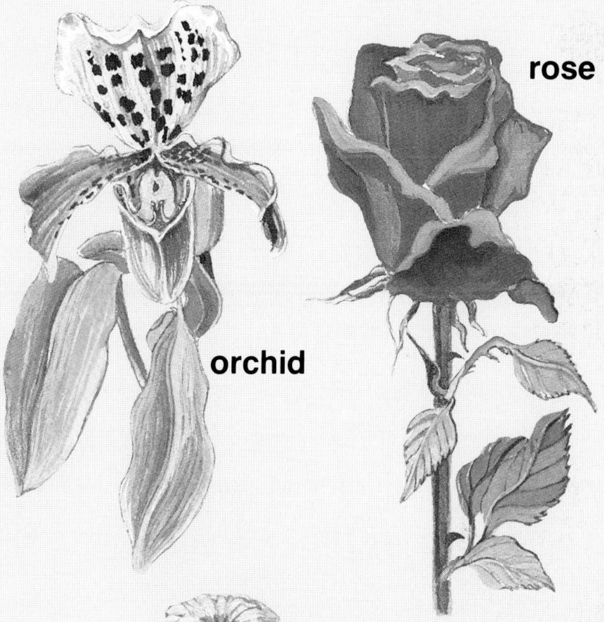

rose

orchid

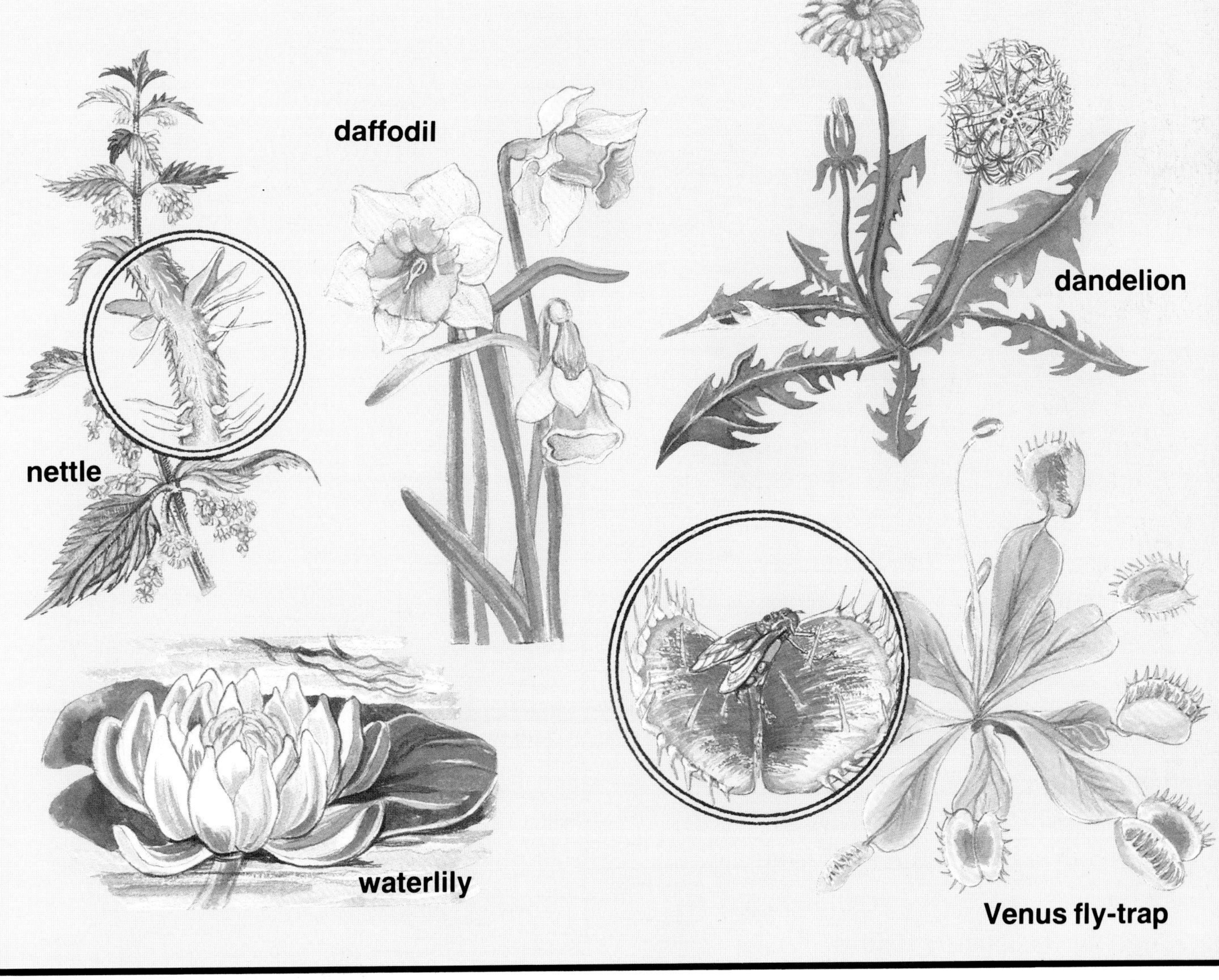

daffodil

dandelion

nettle

waterlily

Venus fly-trap

F Fossil Fox France

Fossil

Fossils are the remains of plants and animals that lived millions of years ago. When the plant or animal died, it was covered with mud. Slowly the mud dried and hardened. The shape of the animal or plant was left in the mud. Fossils show us what plants and animals of long ago looked like.

Some of the fuel we use today comes from fossils. When the plants and animals died they were buried in mud. Layers of mud pressed them down into the earth. They turned into coal or oil. Coal and oil are fossil fuels.

Above: The fossil of a fish.

Fox

Foxes are part of the dog family. They have long pointed noses and bushy tails. Foxes sleep during the day. At night they hunt for small animals and birds. Foxes live in holes under the ground. Their homes are called earths.

This is a red fox. Arctic foxes have white fur to help them to hide in the snow. Fennec foxes live in the desert. Their fur is a sandy colour.

France

France is one of the countries of Europe. It has very good farming land and many French people are farmers. They grow grape vines in the hottest areas and the grapes are made into wine. France makes about one third of all the world's wine.

France is also an industrial country. Iron and steel are made there, and cars are made and sold to other countries.

The capital city of France is Paris. It has many famous museums and art galleries, and the tall Eiffel Tower.

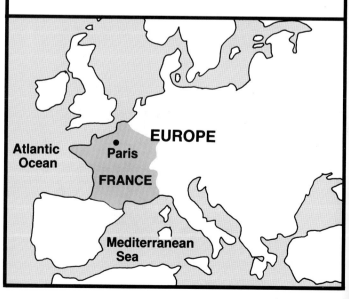

Frog

Frogs can live in water and on land. They are amphibians. They lay their eggs in the water. The eggs (frogspawn) are covered in jelly. Tadpoles grow inside the jelly. When they hatch out of the eggs they look like tiny fish. They breathe through gills. As they get bigger they grow legs. The back legs appear first. Then the tail shrinks. After 12 weeks the tadpoles begin to look like frogs.

Adult frogs have no tails. They breathe through lungs. Frogs hop about on land and eat small insects. They sleep during the winter. Frogs sing with croaks and grunts.

LIFE CYCLE OF THE COMMON FROG

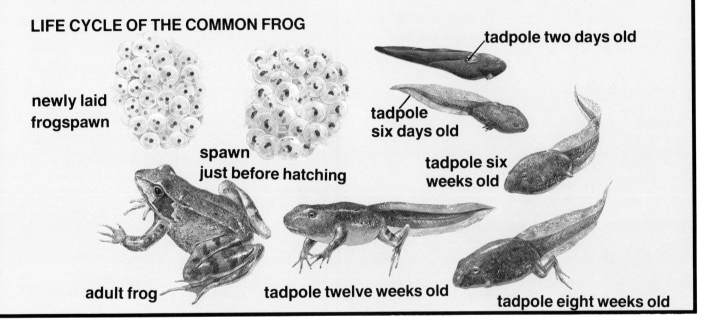

newly laid frogspawn

spawn just before hatching

tadpole two days old

tadpole six days old

tadpole six weeks old

adult frog

tadpole twelve weeks old

tadpole eight weeks old

Fruit

Plants and trees produce fruit. The fruit contains seeds. Apple pips are seeds. Plums and cherries have hard stones inside them. These stones are seeds too. Strawberries have their seeds on the outside of the fruit.

Animals and birds eat fruit. They carry the seeds away in their bodies. Then the seeds pass through their bodies. New plants can grow where the seeds are dropped.

Many fruits are good to eat. They contain vitamins to keep people healthy. Some fruits are not good to eat. They make us sick. They are poisonous.

G Gas Germany Germs

Gas

Gas gives us power. It makes machines work. Cookers, fires, refrigerators and central heating all use gas. Natural gas is a fossil fuel. It is found underground. Like coal and oil, natural gas was made millions of years ago out of plants and animals. Gas comes to our homes through pipelines.

1. A gas field at sea.
2. A gas pipeline.
3. Gas in the kitchen.

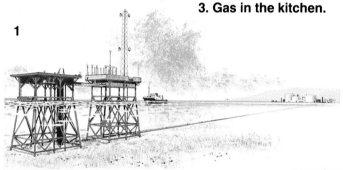

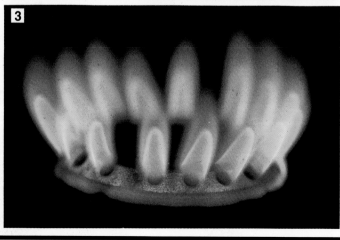

Germany

Germany was divided into two parts in 1949. About 17 million people live in East Germany. Farmers grow cereals, sugar beet and potatoes. There are mines and many factories.

About 57 million people live in West Germany. They grow and make the same things that people do in East Germany. They also make a great deal of wine. In both countries there are many rivers and canals. Goods can travel by water on barges.

West Germany is part of the Common Market. East Germany has links with other countries in eastern Europe.

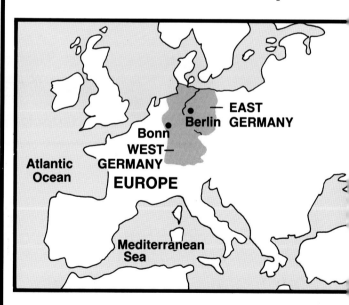

EAST GERMANY
Berlin
Bonn
WEST GERMANY
Atlantic Ocean
EUROPE
Mediterranean Sea

Germs

Germs are tiny living things. They live all around us. We have to use a microscope to see them. Germs grow and spread in warm, damp places. Some germs cause diseases. They give us colds and 'flu. Germs in our mouths make our teeth decay.

Giraffe

Giraffes are the tallest animals. They grow to nearly six metres. They live on the plains of Africa. Their long necks help them reach the tops of trees. They eat the leaves they find there. Giraffes spread their long legs wide when they stoop down to drink. Their long legs help them to gallop very fast if they are frightened. The brown and yellow patterns on their skins help them to hide among the trees. This is called camouflage.

Goat

Wild goats live in rocky places and on mountain slopes. They are excellent climbers. Tame female goats produce good milk. Goat hair can be made into cloth. Goat skins make very good leather.

Gold

Gold is a very expensive metal. Some gold is found inside rocks in the ground. Miners dig out the rocks. Then the rocks are crushed. Only a small amount of gold is found in each rock. Sometimes tiny grains of gold are found in river beds.

Gold is very soft. It can be beaten into shape and moulded. It is often used to make fine jewellery.

Below: This bracelet is made of gold.

G Goldfish Gorilla Grasshopper

Goldfish

Goldfish come from China. They are a beautiful bright orange colour. People breed them especially to produce the orange colour. Wild goldfish are a dull colour. Goldfish live in cold water. They can be kept as pets in aquariums or in garden ponds.

Above: A goldfish swimming.

Gorilla

Gorillas are the largest of the apes. They are very strong but they seldom fight each other. They live peacefully in family groups in the African jungle. During the day they search for food. They eat bamboo shoots, leaves and fruit. At night one gorilla keeps watch, on the ground. The others sleep safely in trees. There are not many gorillas left now. They are in danger of becoming extinct.

Below: Gorillas live mainly on the ground.

Grasshopper

Grasshoppers are jumping insects. They have long back legs to help them jump. Most grasshoppers also have wings for flying.

Male grasshoppers make chirping noises. They do this by rubbing their back legs against their wings. You can often hear them in the grass on a sunny day.

Grasshoppers eat leaves and plants. In Africa there are large grasshoppers called locusts. They destroy many of the farmers' crops.

Gravity

Gravity is a very strong force. It keeps everything on Earth from falling off into space. When you throw a ball into the air, gravity pulls the ball back to Earth. Gravity also keeps the Earth on its path round the Sun. It keeps the Moon on its path round the Earth.

Gravity is very important to us. It holds the Earth's atmosphere in place. The atmosphere is a layer of gases round the Earth. We need these gases to breathe.

Spaceships have to travel very fast to escape the Earth's gravity. In space, astronauts float about in their spaceships. This happens because there is no gravity to hold them down. This makes it very difficult for them to move around in the spaceships.

There is no gravity in space so astronauts float.

Grasslands

Grasslands are large areas of country covered in grass. There are grasslands in Africa. It is hot there and rain falls only in the summer. The grass provides food for many herds of wild animals. Sometimes trees grow with the grass.

Below: These grasslands are in East Africa.

G Great Britain Guinea pig Guitar

Great Britain

Great Britain is an island divided into three countries, England, Scotland and Wales. About 53 million people live there. They speak English, and Wales and Scotland also have their own languages. They are Welsh and Gaelic. These countries, together with Northern Ireland, make up the United Kingdom (UK). The Isle of Man, the Shetland and Orkney Islands and the Channel Islands are also part of the UK. London is the capital city of the UK.

Britain produces coal, iron and steel. Aircraft, ships, cars and parts for machines are made and sold all over the world. Cotton, woollen and plastic goods are made too.

Farmers grow cereals, sugar beet and all kinds of fruit and vegetables on British farms. Some of this is sold abroad too. The UK is part of the Common Market.

Guinea pig

Guinea pigs are small rodents like hamsters and gerbils. The adult guinea pig can grow to about 30 centimetres and can weigh about 436 grams. They have large heads, short legs and have no tails. Their coats can be long or short, smooth or rough. The colour of their coats can be brown, black, white, tan or mixed colours.

Guinea pigs make good pets because they are very easy to care for. A diet of vegetables, crushed oats and bran keeps them healthy.

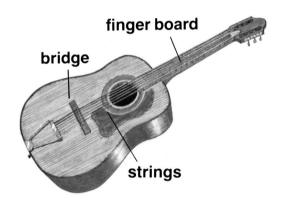

Guitar

A guitar is a musical instrument with six strings. A player plucks the strings with one hand. The other hand presses the strings down. Different notes are made by pressing the strings down on to the fingerboard in different places.

Guitars are used in many kinds of music. Spanish dancers dance to guitar music. Some guitars are used in jazz. Some are used to play classical music. Folk singers often use guitars. Many pop singers use electric guitars.

Hamster   Harrier jump jet   Hedgehog   **H**

Harrier jump jet

Harriers take off and land vertically. They do not need a runway. They can fly up, sideways, backwards or forwards. They can also hover. Harriers use lasers to help in an attack. They have radar warning for defence. They are the world's first military jump jets.

Hedgehog

Hedgehogs have short legs and prickly coats. When they are in danger they curl up into a ball. Their sharp prickles protect them from being eaten by other animals. Hedgehogs feed at night, eating plants, fruit and insects. They sleep throughout the winter.

Hamster

Hamsters are rodents with short stumpy tails. They have long front teeth for gnawing their food. They especially enjoy eating seeds and plants. Wild hamsters live in warm dry places.

Hamsters make good pets. They need to be kept warm. Hamsters sleep during the day. They wake up and feed at night. They are very short-sighted as they do not need to see at night.

H Helicopter Henry VIII Hibernation
High-speed train

Helicopter

Helicopters land and take off vertically. They can also hover in the air. The huge blade on top is called a rotor. It can make the helicopter go forward, or hover, or even fly backwards.

Helicopters are often used for rescuing people in the mountains or from the sea or sea cliffs. Large helicopters can carry very heavy loads.

Henry VIII (1509-1547)

Henry VIII was a very powerful king of England.

When he became king, England's religion was Catholic. The Pope was the head of the church. Henry disagreed with the Pope. He made himself head of the church in England.

Henry married six times. He had one son and two daughters. One of his daughters was Queen Elizabeth I.

Hibernation

To hibernate means to sleep through the winter. Some animals do this because there is not enough food for them in the cold winter months. Snakes coil up in holes in the ground. Frogs bury themselves in mud. Hedgehogs sleep under dead leaves.

During hibernation, animals' bodies grow very cold. When the warm spring sunshine comes, the animals wake up.

High-speed train

Electra is Britain's new electric high-speed train. It is named after a Greek goddess. The new train's top speed is about 220 km per hour. It can travel twice as fast as an ordinary family car.

Hippopotamus Horse Hovercraft **H**

Hippopotamus

The hippopotamus is a large heavy animal with very thick skin. It lives in Africa. For much of the day it lies in muddy rivers. The water and mud help to keep it cool in the hot sunshine. At night, the hippopotamus comes out on to the land to feed. It eats huge amounts of grass and water plants. Large herds of hippopotamus feed together and leave wide paths of bare land behind them.

Horse

Horses have one hoof on each leg. The hoofs can be protected by horseshoes.

Horses have been used for thousands of years. At first they were kept for their milk and meat. Then people learned how to ride them. Horses were also used to pull carts and other loads.

Some horses are bred for racing. They can gallop very fast. Large farm horses are slower but they are strong. Today many people enjoy riding.

Hovercraft

A hovercraft can travel over water and over land. Powerful jet engines push air down out of the bottom of the hovercraft. Then the hovercraft rides on this cushion of air. It does not touch the sea or the land. Propellers push it forward. Large hovercraft can carry many passengers and cars.

H Human body

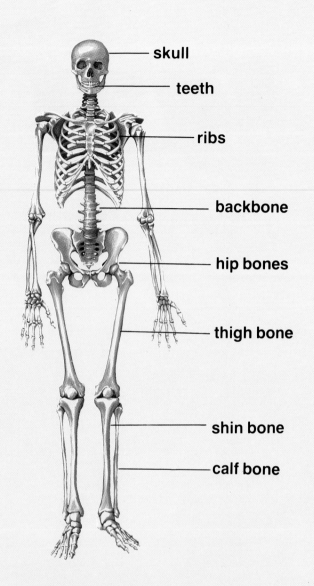

skull

teeth

ribs

backbone

hip bones

thigh bone

shin bone

calf bone

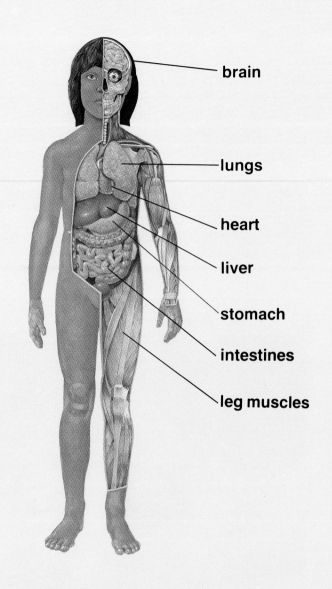

brain

lungs

heart

liver

stomach

intestines

leg muscles

Skeleton

Our bodies are built around a framework of bones. This framework is called a skeleton. It holds our bodies upright. It also protects the organs inside.

There are more than 200 bones in the human body. You can see some of them in this drawing. The skull protects the brain from damage. The backbone keeps us upright. The ribs protect the lungs and heart. The arms, legs and hips are jointed. These joints allow us to move our bodies and walk.

How your body works

This is what your body is like under the skin. It is very complicated. The brain is used for thinking. The lungs enable us to breathe air. The heart pumps blood around the body. The liver cleans out poisons. The bones are covered in muscles which we use to move.

All bodies need food. Food passes from the mouth to the stomach. There it is broken up into a watery mixture. The waste food passes through the intestines and then out of the body.

The five senses

There are nerves all over our bodies. Nerves carry messages to the brain. Some nerves control the movement of the muscles. They help us to move.

Other nerves control our five senses. We learn what is happening around us through our senses. These five senses are: sight, hearing, taste, smell and touch. When you see something, messages travel from the nerves in your eyes to your brain. Your brain tells you what you have seen. The other senses work in the same way.

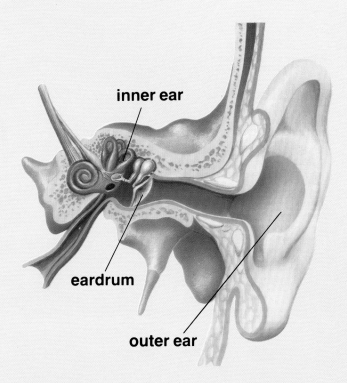

inner ear

eardrum

outer ear

Hearing

Sounds enter our ears and pass along a tube to the eardrum. The eardrum passes the sound to tiny bones inside the ear. Then nerves pass messages about the sound to the brain. The brain tells us what we can hear.

Sight

Light enters our eyes through a small hole in the eyeball. Millions of nerves at the back of the eye pick up messages from the light. They send the messages to the brain. The brain tells us what we can see.

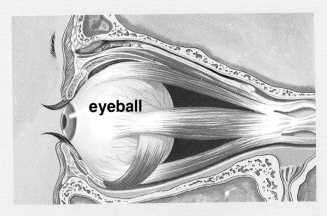

eyeball

Taste, smell, and touch

We taste with our tongues. Different parts pick out different tastes. Nerves in our noses pick up smells in the air.

Nerves in the skin help us to feel. They make us feel pain when we hurt ourselves. They also tell us whether something is hot or cold, rough or smooth, light or heavy.

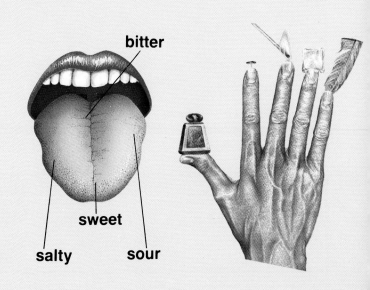

bitter

sweet

salty

sour

I India Insect Iron Italy

India

Eight hundred million people live in India. Hindi is the main language, but there are many others.

In the north of India are the Himalayas, the highest mountains in the world. In the centre and south are low hills and plains. The winds which bring rain are called monsoons.

Indian farmers grow rice, cotton, tea and fruit and vegetables. Factories make goods from cotton and silk, pottery, iron and steel and chemicals. Many people cannot grow enough food to eat. They go to the cities to find jobs. Like cities in other countries, many Indian cities are very crowded.

New Delhi is the capital of India. Calcutta and Bombay are the largest cities. Calcutta has India's first underground railway. Varanasi is the holy city of the Hindu religion.

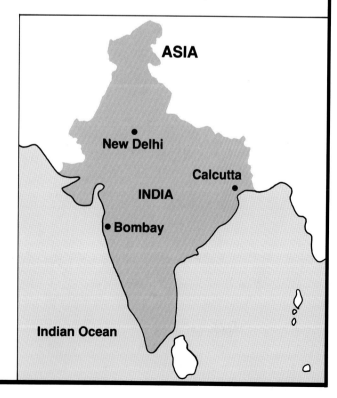

Insect

There are more than a million different kinds of insect in the world. They all have six legs. Their bodies are divided into three separate parts. Many insects have wings for flying. They breathe through air holes in their skin.

Iron

Iron is a metal. It has been used to make tools for thousands of years. When iron is hot it can be bent and shaped. When it cools it is very hard. We say something is 'as hard as iron'.

Italy

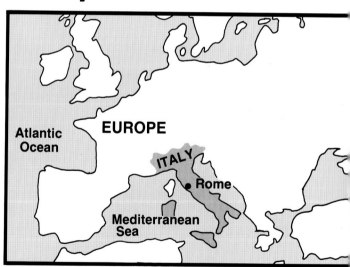

Italy is a long narrow country. It is shaped like a boot. The islands of Sardinia and Sicily belong to Italy.

Northern Italy has many large towns and factories. In Southern Italy the people are poorer. It is hotter and many grapes and olives are grown there. Rome and Florence are two Italian cities with beautiful old buildings.

Japan

Japan is made up of four large islands and many small ones. There are many high mountains. About 50 of them are volcanoes. Earthquakes often happen in Japan.

Today, Japan is one of the richest countries. It makes many cars, radios, televisions and other machines. Tokyo is the capital city of Japan.

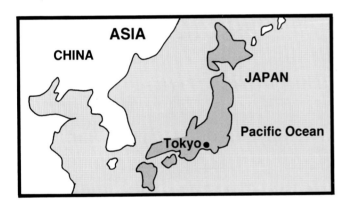

Jellyfish

Jellyfish live in the sea. They have soft bodies. The mouth is underneath the body. They also have long floating tentacles which they use to sting their prey. Jellyfish eat small fish and other sea animals. Sometimes they sting people swimming in the sea.

tentacles

Jesus Christ

Jesus Christ was born in Judea almost 2000 years ago. Christians believe he was the son of God. Jesus taught people about God. He taught them to love each other and not to fight. He healed sick people. The religious leaders did not like his teaching. Jesus was put on a cross to die.

Jumbo jet

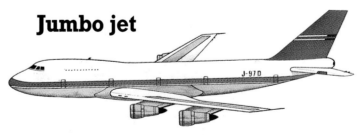

Jumbo jets are the largest passenger planes. They have big wide bodies and powerful jet engines. They can carry about 500 passengers and can fly for long distances. This is a Boeing 747. It was the first jumbo jet to be made.

K Kangaroo Knight

Kangaroo

Kangaroos live in Australia. They have large back legs and hop along very quickly looking for plants to eat. Their long tails help them to balance upright. Some kangaroos are as tall as people.

Baby kangaroos are called joeys. A newborn joey is no bigger than an adult's thumb-nail. It crawls into the pouch on the front of its mother's body. There, it sucks milk and grows bigger. The joey stays in the pouch for about six months. Then it is old enough to hop about and find food.

Right: A kangaroo and a joey.

Knight

Knights lived long ago. They wore heavy suits of armour and carried swords and shields. Knights learned how to fight, how to be good horse-riders and how to hunt. When there was a war, the king gathered the knights together to help him fight.

Sometimes young boys went to live in noblemen's houses to learn how to become knights.

Laboratory Ladybird Lake L

Laboratory

A laboratory is a room where scientists do experiments. Laboratories are full of special scientific equipment. In the picture below you can see a laboratory in a hospital. The people are wearing masks. The masks keep germs away from the things they are studying. Everything must be kept very clean.

Many schools have laboratories. Pupils learn about science and do experiments there.

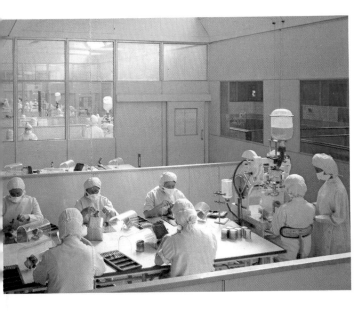

Lake

A lake is an area of water with land all around it. Many lakes, like this one, are found in valleys between mountains.

When rain falls on the mountains, it runs down in streams. The streams flow into lakes. Small lakes are often used for sailing and fishing. Some lakes are huge. Large ships can sail through the deep Great Lakes in North America.

Ladybird

Ladybirds are a kind of beetle. They have hard wing-cases covered in spots. Some ladybirds are red. Some are yellow. The bright colours warn birds that ladybirds are unpleasant to eat.

Ladybirds lay eggs which hatch into larvae. The larvae turn into ladybirds. Ladybirds are very useful in our gardens. They eat greenfly and other insects which destroy plants.

L Laser Leonardo da Vinci Library

Laser

A laser is a strong beam of a special kind of light. Some lasers can cut metal. Some are used in eye operations. The laser beam burns a tiny part of the damaged eye to stop it bleeding. A laser has also been used to measure the distance to the Moon. The laser light was beamed from Earth to the Moon. Scientists measured how long it took to get there.

Leonardo da Vinci (1452-1519)

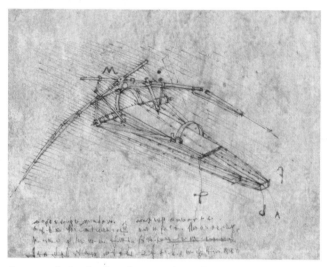

Leonardo's design for an aircraft.

Leonardo da Vinci was one of the most brilliant men who has ever lived. He was an artist, a scientist, a musician and a mathematician. He painted one of the most famous pictures in the world. It is called the 'Mona Lisa'. He made fine drawings and sculptures. He designed buildings and machines. He designed an aircraft long before anyone was able to build one.

Library

A library is a place where books are stored. People borrow books from libraries. Schools have libraries and many towns have public libraries too.

Information is also stored in libraries, on film. The film is called microfiche. It takes up less space than books.

Lifeboat   Light   Lincoln   **L**

Lifeboat

Lifeboats are used to rescue people in danger at sea. Lifeboat crews are very brave. They take their boats out into stormy seas. This is a deep-sea lifeboat. It is made so that it does not sink even if it turns upside down.

Light

Light travels in waves. Light waves travel very, very fast. In the daytime we receive light from the Sun. Sunlight is made up of many colours. We see these colours when there is a rainbow in the sky. A rainbow is made when sunlight falls on raindrops in the air. The raindrops break up the light into its separate colours.

At night we need lamps to give us light. We use electric lights to make our homes and cities bright even on the darkest night. The lights in this picture are in New York.

Lincoln (1809-1865)

Abraham Lincoln was a great American President. There were many slaves in America and Lincoln wanted the slaves to be free. The people who disagreed with him formed an army and fought against Lincoln's army in the American Civil War. Lincoln's army won. A few days after the fighting Lincoln was shot while he was sitting in a theatre.

L Liner Lion Lizard

Liner

Liners are large passenger ships. Many people used to travel to other countries on liners. Now most people travel by plane instead.

Today, liners are mostly used for holiday cruises. They carry hundreds of passengers and are like floating hotels. Liners have their own shops and cinemas. Some have swimming-pools on the deck. At night there are dances and parties. Passengers sleep in small rooms called cabins.

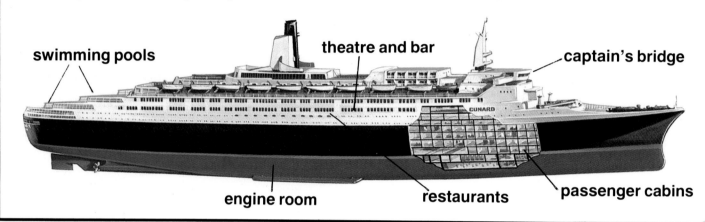

swimming pools

theatre and bar

captain's bridge

engine room

restaurants

passenger cabins

Lion

Lions are members of the cat family. Most lions live in Africa but there are a few in India. A male lion has long hair round its face. This is called a mane. Lions live in groups called prides. Each pride has one or two males and several female lions. These are called lionesses and they do the hunting. They kill zebras and other animals to eat.

Lizard

Lizards are reptiles. They have scaly skins and are cold blooded. There are many different kinds. All lizards can climb and some can swim. A few can even glide through the air. Some lizards lay eggs. Others give birth to live babies.

This lizard is warming its body in the sunshine. It can run faster when it is warm. When it sees an insect, it darts out and catches it. At night it hides in holes or under stones.

Magnet

Magnets are made of iron or steel. They can pull other pieces of iron or steel towards them. Small magnets can pick up things like pins and nails. The pins and nails stick to the magnet. Large magnets are very powerful. They can pick up heavy loads. A large magnet is used to pick pieces of metal out of coal.

Mammals

Mammals are warm-blooded animals. Many mammals have warm fur or hair on their bodies. They all feed their young on milk. Baby mammals grow inside the mother's body. They live in her womb until they are ready to be born. Human beings are mammals. Whales are mammals that live in the sea.

Medicine

For thousands of years people have made all sorts of medicines to try to heal themselves. Many medicines were made from plants and herbs. Herbal medicines are still used today. Some people think they are safer to use than new medicines which are made from chemicals.

Some medicines are pills or liquids. We swallow them. Others are ointments that we rub on to our bodies. We hope the medicine will heal us.

If we feel ill and we do not know what is wrong we go to a doctor. A doctor has studied medicine for many years.

Meteorite

Meteors are rocks moving around in space. Sometimes they enter the Earth's atmosphere. Most meteors burn up in the atmosphere but some very large ones do not burn up completely. They land on Earth. Then they are called meteorites. This huge hole was made by a meteorite.

Microscope

Microscopes make tiny things look larger. This microscope has a mirror at the bottom. The mirror passes light up to a small piece of glass called a slide. A tiny object is on the slide. The light then passes through a special piece of glass called a lens. This makes the object on the slide look larger. When you look into a microscope you can see the object very clearly.

Monkey

There are many different kinds of monkey. They all have hands and feet that can hold and grasp. They use them to climb trees.

Most monkeys live in forests. They climb in the trees looking for leaves and fruit to eat.

All monkeys have tails. Some can use their tails like an extra arm. They swing from the trees holding on with their tails.

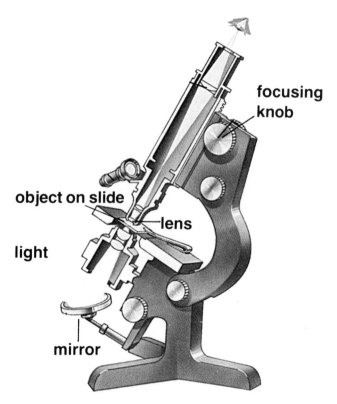

focusing knob

object on slide

lens

light

mirror

Milk

All female mammals produce milk for their young to drink. The milk we buy in bottles and cartons comes from cows. Cows' milk is also used to make butter, cream and cheese.

Moon landing

Mosque

A mosque is a building where Muslims pray to Allah (God). Muslims follow the teachings of Muhammad. Their holy book is the Koran. The Koran is read in the mosque.

Inside a mosque there is a special place showing the direction of the holy city, Mecca. Muhammad was born in Mecca. When Muslims pray they bow down and face Mecca. Muslims pray five times every day.

In 1969, people landed on the Moon for the first time. A giant American rocket took three astronauts close to the Moon. Then two of them climbed into a small spacecraft called the Lunar Module. It landed on the Moon.

The two astronauts were called Neil Armstrong and Edwin Aldrin. They wore spacesuits and carried air to breathe. People weigh very little on the Moon because there is no gravity. It was difficult for the astronauts to walk. They collected Moon rocks to bring back to Earth. They also did experiments. Then the Lunar Module took them back to the spaceship.

Other astronauts have been to the Moon. Some used a Moon buggy like the one in the picture. It made travelling easier.

Left: The Moon buggy on the Moon.

M Moth Motorbike Mountain

Moth

A moth is very like a butterfly. It is often difficult to tell them apart. But most moths fly only at night and they are less colourful than butterflies.

Some moths eat leaves and plants. Clothes moth grubs like to eat holes in clothes stored in cupboards.

Many moths are attracted to light. You can sometimes see them fluttering around lights on summer evenings.

Motorbike

Motorbikes have two wheels and an engine. The back wheel is usually driven by a chain from the engine. Some motorbikes go very fast. They are used for racing. Traffic police often use motorbikes. Motorbikes are smaller than cars so they can get through busy traffic quickly.

Mountain

Mountains are high rocky places. The Earth is covered in a layer of rocks. Over millions of years some of these rocks have been pushed up to form mountains. It is icy cold on high mountains. Few animals and plants can live there. Some mountains are under the sea. Many small islands are the tops of underwater mountains.

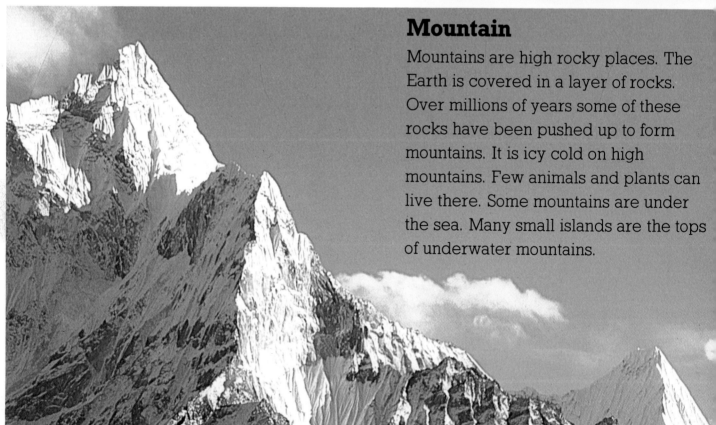

Above: The harvest mouse lives in the fields.

Mouse

A mouse is a small rodent. It gnaws its food with long front teeth. The house mouse lives in houses and barns. It is a pest because it eats crops and carries diseases. This tiny harvest mouse lives in fields. It builds its nest high up among the plant stems.

Mozart (1756-1791)

Wolfgang Amadeus Mozart was born in Austria. When he was four he was already a very good musician. When he was only six he composed music and played in concerts. For the rest of his short life he composed music. It is some of the greatest music ever written. Mozart wrote wonderful operas and symphonies, but he lived and died in great poverty.

Muhammad (570-632)

Muhammad was born in the city of Mecca in Arabia. When he was a young man he had a vision telling him to teach people about God. Muhammad founded the religion of Islam. His followers are called Muslims. Their holy book is called the Koran.

Below: Muslims visiting their holy city of Mecca.

M Museum Mushroom Music

Museum

Museums are places where interesting things from the past are put on show. People visit museums to look at these things. Many museums show you how people lived in the past. Some tell you about fossils, plants and animals. Some show you what scientists have found out about the world.

Music

Music is a pattern of sound played on instruments or sung by people. The different sounds are called notes. Music can be written down using special signs to show these notes. In the picture you can see the first few notes of a piece of music.

Mushroom

Mushrooms are fungi. Fungi are very strange plants. They do not have roots, stems or leaves. Mushrooms begin as little threads under the ground. Then the threads grow into mushrooms. They break through the soil. The flat tops open like little umbrellas.

Mushrooms are good to eat. Toadstools look like mushrooms but some of them are deadly poisonous. So are many other fungi. You must never eat fungi when you do not know what they are.

Napoleon (1769-1821)

Napoleon Bonaparte was a great French leader and soldier. He became Emperor of France. His army captured many countries.

Napoleon's last great battle was the Battle of Waterloo. His army was finally defeated and Napoleon was sent away to live on a lonely island called Saint Helena. He was kept there as a prisoner until he died a few years later.

Newspaper

In newspapers we read about what is happening all over the world. People called reporters find out the news and write about it. The most interesting reports are chosen for printing. Then thousands of copies of the paper are printed on a large machine called a press. The newspapers are then delivered to our shops.

Many papers come out every day. Everyone has to work very fast to produce them.

Below: Newspapers from many countries.

O Oasis Octopus Oil

Oasis

An oasis is a place in the desert where you can find water. The water comes from wells and underground rivers. Travellers and their animals drink at the oasis. Trees and plants grow there. Sometimes desert towns are built around a large oasis.

Octopus

The octopus lives in the sea. It has eight long tentacles like waving arms. It uses them to catch crabs, lobsters and other shellfish. The octopus moves by crawling along the sea bed. It can also swim. It does this by shooting water out of its body. The jet of water pushes it along. It can also squirt out black inky liquid which clouds the water. This hides the octopus from its enemies.

Oil

Oil is a very important fossil fuel. It began as the remains of tiny sea creatures and plants that lived millions of years ago. They slowly turned into oil. Some oil is found underground. Some is found under the sea bed. The things in the bottom picture are made from oil.

oil rig

oil refinery ▼

oil products

Above: The Olympic Games in Los Angeles.

Olympic Games

The first Olympic Games were held by the ancient Greeks. They were held in a place called Olympia. Now the Games are held every four years, each time in a different country. Sportsmen and women from all over the world take part. Almost every kind of sport can be seen.

The Games are opened by lighting the Olympic flame with a burning torch. The torch is lit in Greece and carried to the Games by a team of runners.

Opera

Operas tell stories using music and singing. They are performed on stage. An orchestra in front of the stage plays the music. The singers wear costumes and make-up. They have to be good actors and very fine singers.

Right: An opera singer in 'Don Juan' by Verdi.

O Orchestra

Orchestra

An orchestra is a large group of musicians playing together. They are led by a conductor.

There are four families of musical instruments in an orchestra. The string instruments all look alike but they are different sizes. They are played with bows. Woodwind and brass instruments are played by blowing air into them. Percussion instruments are played by hitting or striking them.

Each group of instruments sits in a special place in the orchestra. Look carefully at the photograph. Can you count how many instruments of each group there are in this orchestra?

double basses

first violins

cello

Woodwind

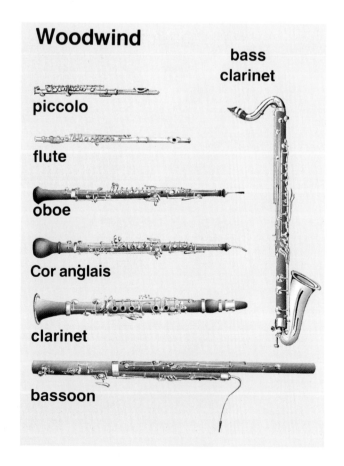

piccolo

flute

oboe

Cor anglais

clarinet

bassoon

bass clarinet

Brass

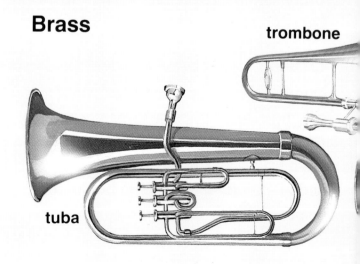

trombone

tuba

percussion

odwind

brass

violas

second violins

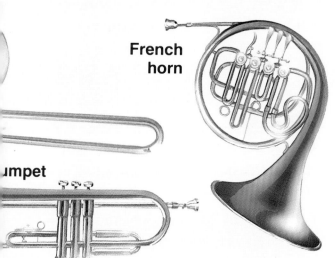

French horn

umpet

Strings

violin

viola

cello

double bass

Percussion

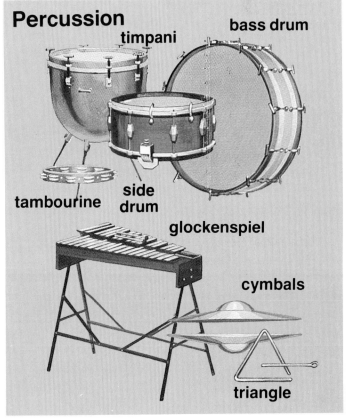

timpani

bass drum

tambourine

side drum

glockenspiel

cymbals

triangle

O   Ostrich Owl Oxygen

Ostrich

Ostriches are the largest birds in the world. They live in Africa. They cannot fly but they can run very fast. Ostriches eat plants and insects. The females lay their eggs together in hollows. They take it in turns to look after the eggs. Ostriches often live with zebras and other large animals. They are so tall that they can see when danger is coming. They warn the other animals of the danger.

Owl

Owls are birds of prey. They hunt at night. They fly very quietly in the dark. Their large eyes and sharp ears help them to find their prey. Then they swoop down to catch a small animal or bird. Owls can swallow whole rats and mice. They eat the meat and spit out the fur and bones. You can recognise owls by their short stumpy shape, big round eyes and hooting voice.

Oxygen

Oxygen is a gas. You cannot see it, taste it or smell it. It is in the air all around us. All animals need oxygen to breathe. We breathe it in through our lungs. We could not live if we had no oxygen to breathe.

Painting Palace **P**

Painting

From earliest times people have enjoyed painting pictures. This painting of an animal was made by cave people. It was found on a cave wall. The girl on the right is painting a picture of the scene around her. The other picture shows the death of a Danish explorer. Artists use many different kinds of paint. Water-colours, oils and poster paints are three of the most popular kinds.

Above: A girl painting the scene around her.

Above: A painting made by cave people.

Above: The death of the explorer Vitus Bering.

Palace

Palaces are the homes of important people such as kings and queens. They are usually large and beautiful buildings. Most palaces contain fine furniture and paintings. Many of them have lovely gardens all around them. This is a picture of Chambord Palace in France. The palace is surrounded by a very large park.

Above: Chambord Palace in France.

P Panda Paper Penguin Piano

Penguin

Penguins are birds but they cannot fly. On land they hop and slide about clumsily. In the sea they are excellent swimmers and divers. Penguins live in the frozen land of Antarctica.

Panda

Giant pandas are related to bears. They are large animals with black and white fur. They live in bamboo forests in China and Tibet and eat bamboo shoots. Pandas are now very rare. A few are kept in zoos. People hope that these zoo pandas will breed. Then the number of pandas in the world will increase. If pandas do not breed, they may become extinct.

Piano

Pianos are large musical instruments. You play them by pressing down keys on the keyboard. When you press a key it moves a small hammer inside the piano. The hammer hits a string. This makes a musical note.

Paper

Most paper is made from trees. It is made in factories called paper mills. First the trees are broken up into wood pulp. The pulp is pressed and dried. Then it is cut into sheets of paper. Every day thousands of trees are cut down to make paper. Think of how much paper we use to write on and to make books and newspapers. It is an enormous amount. Paper is used for wrapping and packing things too.

Picasso (1881-1973)

Pablo Picasso is one of the most famous modern artists. He was born in Spain but he spent most of his life in France. He made many drawings, paintings and sculptures.

By the time he was ten years old, he was already a fine artist. At first he painted beautiful sad pictures in pale blue and pink colours. Then he experimented with bright colours and strange shapes. He painted the picture below in this way. The people look very different from photographs.

Below: 'The Three Dancers' by Picasso.

Pig

Farmyard pigs are related to fierce wild boars. They have thick bristly skins. Their feet have hoofs and are divided into two toes. Pigs use their strong snouts to dig in the ground for food. They eat anything they can find. Pigs provide us with a great amount of food. Pork, bacon, ham and sausage meat all come from pigs.

Piranha

Piranha fish live in South American rivers. They are small and very fierce. Piranhas swim in large groups and kill their prey with razor sharp teeth. They can even kill large animals that swim or wade in the river.

P Planets

Luna 16

Planets

Scientists have now begun to explore the planets which are near Earth. Men have landed on the Moon. They did experiments and brought back pieces of Moon rock to Earth.

Robot explorers have also landed on the Moon. This picture shows a Russian robot called Luna 16. It scooped up soil from the Moon and brought it back to Earth for scientists to study.

Other robot explorers have travelled far into space. Some have landed on Mars. Others have sent back pictures of Mercury, Venus, Jupiter and Saturn. Voyager spacecraft have been sent to study the planets furthest away from Earth. No sign of life has been found on any of these planets.

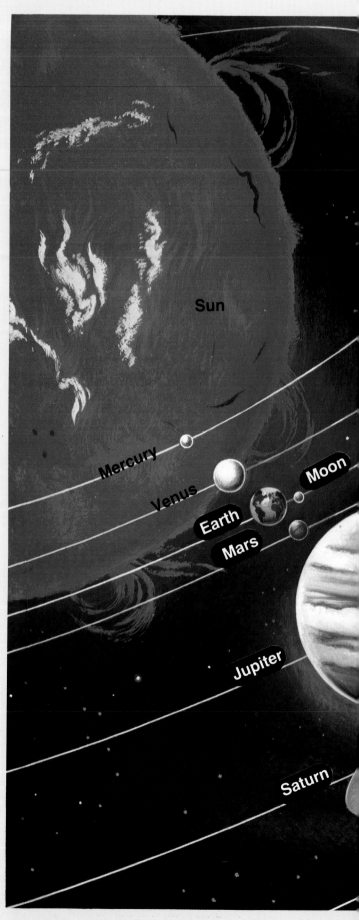
Sun
Mercury
Venus
Earth
Moon
Mars
Jupiter
Saturn

Uranus

Neptune

Pluto

Our Sun is a hot shining star. Nine planets travel around it.

Mercury and Venus are closest to the Sun so they are very hot. The Earth is the third planet from the Sun. It is round like a ball. It has a rocky surface and is surrounded by a layer of air. The Earth takes one year to travel round the Sun. Mars is rocky. It is covered in red dust. Jupiter and Saturn are enormous balls of liquid and gas. Uranus, Neptune and Pluto are far from the Sun so they are very cold. We know very little about them. The Voyager spacecraft above was sent to explore these distant planets.

Plants

There are plants all over the world, on land and in water. Most land plants have roots, stems and leaves. Roots draw water from the soil. Leaves use sunlight to make the plant's food. Many plants have flowers. Some plants are tiny and some are huge. Giant redwood trees are the largest plants.

Plastic

The first plastic was made about 120 years ago. Now scientists have found out how to make many different kinds. All plastics can be moulded and shaped. Our homes and schools are full of things made from plastic. You can see some of them in this picture.

Poison

Poisons damage our bodies and make us ill. Some can even kill people. Some snakes inject poison into their prey. Some toadstools are deadly poisonous. Many berries are poisonous to human beings. Food that has gone bad can poison us. Many chemicals can harm or kill us if we swallow them.

Pompeii

Pompeii was a Roman city. It was destroyed about 1900 years ago. A volcano called Mount Vesuvius erupted and buried it in hot ash. Now the ash has been dug away. You can visit Pompeii and see the ancient houses. You can see some of the people who died there. The shapes of their bodies have been found in the hard ash.

Pottery

People learned how to make pottery thousands of years ago. They shaped wet mud or clay into bowls and jugs. When they baked them the clay hardened.

Archaeologists have found all kinds of pottery. The Chinese made porcelain, which comes from a special kind of clay. Some pottery is beautifully decorated. Greek pottery has pictures of gods and goddesses and animals on it. The pots tell us about people's lives.

Printing Puppet Pyramids P

Printing

All our books, magazines and newspapers are printed. Blank paper is fed into huge machines called printing presses. The machines print words and pictures on to the paper. They can print many copies very quickly. Before printing was invented all books were written by hand. It was slow and difficult work. There were very few books in the world at that time.

Puppet

Puppets are little figures of people or animals that can be made to move. They are used to tell stories and act plays. Some puppets are worked by long strings. People pull the strings and speak the puppets' voices. Some puppets fit onto your hand. Your fingers make them work. They are called glove puppets. The puppet in the picture above is tiny, one finger fits inside it and makes it work.

Pyramids

Above: The Great Pyramid at Giza in Egypt.

Long ago, Egyptians buried their kings and queens in tombs called pyramids. The pyramids were made of stone and had triangular sides. Inside there were rooms and passages. The kings and queens were buried with all their treasure. Their bodies were specially wrapped to stop them rotting. These wrapped bodies are called mummies.

Some pyramids can still be seen. They are more than 4000 years old.

Q Quadruped Quail Quayside

Quadruped

A quadruped is an animal with four legs. All animals that have four legs are called quadrupeds. This springbok is a quadruped. It uses its four legs to help it run away from enemies. It can run very fast.

Quail

Quails are small brown and black birds. Their colour helps them to lie hidden on the ground. Quails do not fly much. Some people like to shoot quails because they are good to eat.

Quayside

Above: Boats are tied up at the quayside when they are not being used.

A quayside is a landing place for boats. The boats are tied up there safely when they are not being used.

Holiday-makers in pleasure boats can use this small quayside. You will often find a quayside like this in a fishing village.

Fishing boats sail from the quay. When they return, the crews unload their fish on to the quayside. Then they tie their boats to the quay until they need to use them again.

Some quaysides are large. Big ships can load and unload their cargo there.

Rabbit Radio Recorder Reptile R

Rabbit

Rabbits live all over the world. They have long front teeth but they are not rodents. They eat plants. Rabbits build underground homes called burrows. Large numbers of rabbits live together in each burrow. This jack rabbit lives in deserts in America.

Radio

You cannot see or hear radio waves but they are all around us. They travel very fast. They are used to send radio programmes and messages. Ships and planes use radios to speak to people on land. The police use pocket radios.

This disc jockey is making a radio programme. He speaks into a microphone. It turns his voice into radio waves. Our radios pick up these waves and turn them into sounds we can hear.

Recorder

Recorders are woodwind instruments. They are pipes with seven finger-holes and a thumb-hole. You blow into them to make music. Different sounds are made by covering different holes with your fingers.

Reptile

Reptiles are cold-blooded animals with scaly skins. They breathe through lungs. Crocodiles, snakes, tortoises and lizards are all reptiles. Some lay eggs. Some give birth to live babies. They can all live on land.

The first reptiles lived on Earth millions of years ago. Dinosaurs were very early reptiles.

R River Robin Robot

River

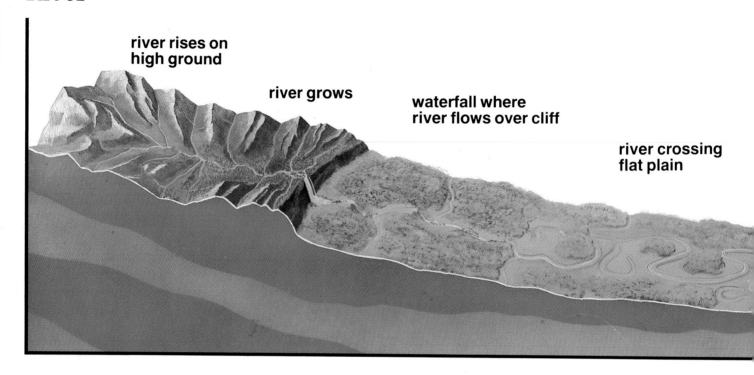

river rises on high ground

river grows

waterfall where river flows over cliff

river crossing flat plain

Robin

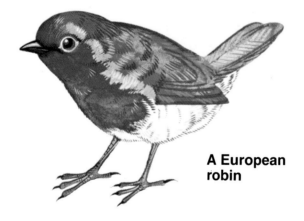

A European robin

The robins that live in Europe are small. When they are fully grown they have red feathers on their breasts. Their pointed beaks help them to pick up insects and crumbs. Many robins live in gardens. Each robin has its own piece of land. It chases away any other robin. American robins are larger. They have breast feathers that are a rusty red.

Robot

Robots are machines that can do some of the things people do. Some robots in factories build machines and cars. A computer tells them what to do. Robot explorers have landed on some planets, and have found out information. In stories and films, robots look, talk and think like people. No one has yet built a robot like this.

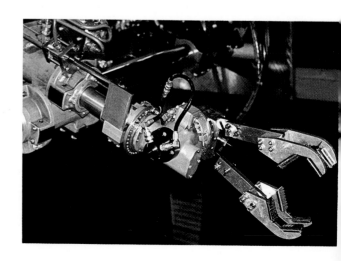

Rocket Rockets Rodents R

Rivers are made from rain water. Rain falls high up on hills and mountains. Some of it turns to ice. Rain and melted ice run down in streams. The streams join together to make rivers. The rivers flow on down to the sea. Some rivers are small. Some are huge. Large ships can sail along them.

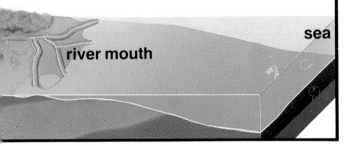

Rocket

The Rocket was one of the first railway engines. It was driven by steam. An inventor called George Stephenson built it about 150 years ago. It travelled at about 47 kilometres per hour. This seemed very fast then.

Rockets

Rockets carry spacecraft up through the Earth's atmosphere. They are very powerful. Space rockets are launched from towers called launching pads. They are full of fuel so they are very heavy. When the fuel burns, it makes a hot gas. The gas shoots out of the rocket and pushes it upwards.

Rodents

Rodents gnaw their food with long front teeth. These teeth never stop growing. Rodents have to keep them short by gnawing at plants and wood. Rats, mice, squirrels, beavers and hamsters are all rodents.

S Salmon Salt Satellite Sculpture

Salmon

Salmon are beautiful silvery fish. They spend most of their adult life in the sea. They swim back to rivers to lay their eggs. Often they swim back to the river where they were born. Nobody knows how salmon do this.

Salmon sometimes leap up small waterfalls on their long journey back up the river. Then they lay their eggs in the river. The eggs hatch into tiny fish. These live in the river for several years. When they have grown large enough, they swim all the way down to the sea.

Salt

Many people put salt on their food. In some places salt is found in the ground. Machines are used to dig it out. The sea is full of salt. These people are collecting salt from shallow pools of sea water. The sun dries up the water and the salt is left behind.

Satellite

A satellite is a machine which is taken into space by rockets and left to circle the Earth. As it travels round it sends messages back to Earth.

Some satellites study the weather. Some send telephone messages. Others send television pictures. The pictures travel up to the satellites and they bounce the pictures down to other parts of the world.

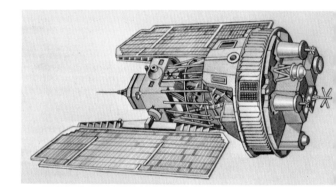

Sculpture

Sculptures are shaped or carved out of wood or stone or other materials. They are not flat like paintings. You can walk right round them. Many sculptures are models or portraits of people. This is a sculpture of the head of a Greek god. It was made thousands of years ago.

Sea

Almost three-quarters of the Earth is covered by sea. That is why the Earth is sometimes called the Blue Planet.

There are rocky mountains and steep valleys under the sea, just like those on land. Many animals and plants live in the sea. Some even live in the deepest parts where it is very cold and dark.

For thousands of years people have crossed the sea in boats. Now we are beginning to find out what life is like under the sea. Scientists explore the sea bed in special diving machines. Some scientists are trying to find out if people can live under the sea.

Seagull

There are many different gulls. They all live near the seashore. They look for shellfish and worms to eat. Seagulls are very good gliders. Many of them have harsh, shrieking voices.

Seahorse

Seahorses are strange fish. They can hold on to seaweed with their tails. They swim upright and eat small fish. Female seahorses lay eggs in the water. The male puts them in his pouch and hatches them out.

Seaweed

Seaweed plants grow in sea water. Some are green and others are brown or red. Their leaves are thick and rubbery. They do not have any flowers. Seaweed can be used to improve soil. It is a fertiliser.

S Secretary Seed Shakespeare Shark

Secretary

Secretaries work in offices. They type letters, arrange meetings and organise the office.

Many offices now have word processors as well as typewriters. A word processor has a screen, like a computer. You can see what you have typed on the screen. Then it is printed on paper.

Seed

Plants grow from seeds. Inside each seed there is a new plant waiting to grow (1). When seeds have enough warmth, water and soil, the seed covering splits open. A small root grows down into the soil (2). Then shoots grow up towards the light (3). They break through the soil and develop into green leaves (4).

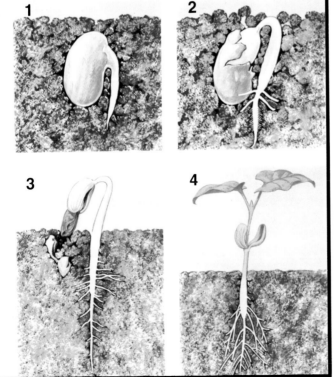

Shakespeare (1564-1616)

William Shakespeare is the world's most famous playwright. He was born in Stratford-upon-Avon. He went to London to be an actor and writer. He wrote about 38 plays and many poems. Some of his plays are funny. They are comedies. Some are sad, and are called tragedies. Others are about history.

Shark

Sharks are large fish. They live in all the oceans of the world. Most sharks are flesh-eaters and some will attack people. Some sharks lay eggs. Others give birth to live young.

Sheep

Sheep are farm animals. They are usually kept in large flocks on hillsides. They eat grass. Sheepdogs are often used to help gather the sheep together. Sheep are very useful animals. Each year their heavy coats are cut off and made into wool. The lamb and mutton we eat comes from sheep.

Shells

Some animals have soft bodies inside a hard shell. You can often find the shells of sea creatures on the seashore. Cockles, scallops and mussels live in the sea. They have two shells. Winkles have one coiled shell, like a snail.

mussels

winkles

cockles

scallops

Shrimp

Shrimps are small shellfish. Some live in the sea. Some live in rivers. They eat small water creatures. The shrimp has a hard jointed shell. It has ten legs. Some of these legs work like paddles to help the shrimp to swim. Shrimps are very good to eat.

Skylab

Skylab was a large American spacecraft. It was launched by a rocket, but it was damaged when it took off. Three astronauts went up in another spacecraft to mend it. Skylab was the first space laboratory. The nine astronauts on board did many experiments. Mice, spiders and fish also travelled in Skylab. Scientists used them to learn about living in space.

S Snail Snake South America

Snail

Some snails live in water. Some live on land. You can often see snails eating plants in the garden. They have hard round shells. Their eyes are on the ends of stalks on top of their heads. Snails move along on one soft foot. The foot produces slime which helps the snail move over the ground. When a snail is in danger it hides inside its shell.

Snake

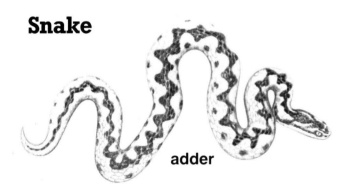

adder

Snakes are reptiles. They have no legs so they slither along the ground. They can move fast. All snakes hatch from eggs. They have jaws that can open very wide. This helps them to eat animals. Their bodies are scaly.

Many snakes are very dangerous. Some poison their prey by biting them with their fangs. Some kill their prey by squeezing them to death.

This is an adder. It is the only poisonous snake found in Britain.

South America

South America is made up of many different countries. It is joined to North America by a narrow strip of land. Part of South America is covered in huge tropical forests. The great River Amazon flows through these hot, wet forests. There are very high mountains all along the west coast of South America called the Andes.

Most of the world's coffee is grown in South America. There are also large cattle ranches. The cattle provide beef for people to eat.

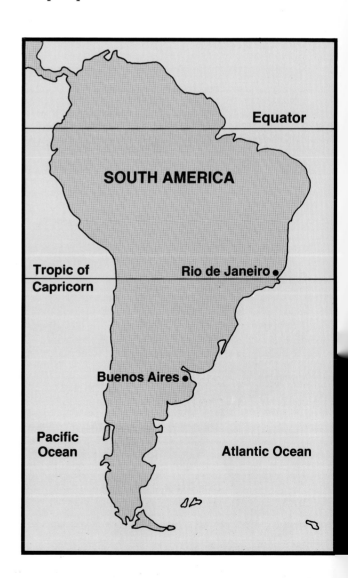

Equator

SOUTH AMERICA

Tropic of Capricorn

Rio de Janeiro •

Buenos Aires •

Pacific Ocean

Atlantic Ocean

Space Shuttle

The Space Shuttle is part spacecraft and part aeroplane. A rocket carries it up into space. Then the Space Shuttle circles round the Earth. The pilot brings it down to land on Earth. It lands like a glider without using an engine. The Shuttle can be used over and over again to fly into space. It was built in the United States of America and first launched in 1981.

Spain

Spain is a country in southern Europe. It is part of the Common Market. The south of Spain is very near the African coast. In summer it is very hot. People go there for their holidays.

Grapes are grown in Spain. They are made into wine and sherry. Olives and oranges are grown there too. Spain is famous for its bullfights and lively dancing to guitar music. The capital city of Spain is Madrid.

Spider

Spiders are not insects. Insects have six legs, but spiders have eight. All spiders eat insects. Many of them spin fine silk webs to catch their prey.

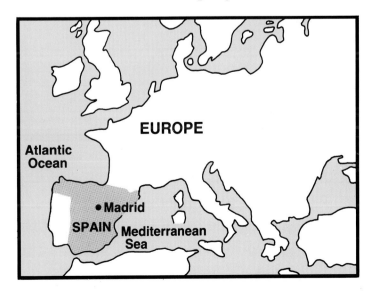

S Sport

Baseball

Baseball is played between two teams of nine players. The pitcher throws the ball. The striker hits i
Then the striker tries to run round as many bases as possible before the ball is returned.

Soccer

Soccer is played between two teams of eleven players. A goal is scored when the ball is kicked or headed between the opponents' goal posts.

Gymnastics

Gymnasts perform exercises on special equipment. They need to be strong and very graceful. This girl is standing on her hands on a very narrow beam of wood. Many gymnasts take part in competitions. The judges give marks for grace, rhythm and skill.

Cricket

Cricket is played between two teams of eleven players. When one team bats, the other team fields. The bowler in this picture has bowled the ball to the batsman. The batsman has hit it as far as he can. He scores a run if he can reach the other wicket before the ball is returned. The team scoring the most runs is the winner.

Horse racing

Racehorses are specially bred and trained to take part in races. Their riders are called jockeys. Some races are run over flat ground. In other races the horses have to jump over high hedges and wide ditches. Many people go to race meetings just to watch.

Skiing

Skiers travel across snow on long narrow skis. Competitions are held to find the fastest skiers. They ski down steep hillsides. Some skiers go ski jumping. They ski down long ramps and jump off the end into the air.

Swimming

Swimmers race each other through the water as quickly or as gracefully as they can. This swimmer is doing the butterfly stroke.

Tennis

Tennis is played on a special court. Two people play in a singles match. They stand on either side of the net and hit the ball to each other with rackets.

S Squirrel Stagecoach

Squirrel

Squirrels are rodents with bushy tails. They live in trees. Their sharp claws and strong back legs help them to climb quickly. Squirrels eat nuts and, sometimes, birds' eggs. They do great damage to trees by eating the bark. The grey squirrel is often seen in parks and woods. There are very few red squirrels in Britain now.

Stagecoach

Stagecoaches used to take people from place to place before cars and trains were invented. The passengers sat in the carriage. Sometimes they sat on the roof. The roads were rough and bumpy so stagecoaches were slow and uncomfortable. The horses had to be changed when they became tired. The places where they were changed were called stages.

Stamps

Stamps are stuck on letters and parcels. They show that you have paid for the letter or parcel to be posted. Stamps are produced by countries all over the world. They are very attractive. Many people collect them.

Stars

Stars are clouds of gas and dust in space. They shine because they are very hot. Our Sun is a star. It gives us our light and heat.

There are millions of stars in the universe. They are very far away. We can see only a few of them in the sky at night. Huge radio telescopes can pick up signals from stars too far away for us to see.

Station

Stations are places where trains or buses stop. Large stations, like this one in Germany, are very busy places. There are many long platforms. Hundreds of trains stop there every day. Most stations have places where you can eat and drink. There are shops where you can buy books and magazines for your journey. Noticeboards and loudspeakers tell the passengers where they can find their train.

S Submarine Sundial

Submarine

Submarines are boats that travel under the sea. They are specially built to dive under the water. Sea water is let into tanks in the submarine. This makes it heavy, so it dives down. Engines drive the submarine forwards. Then the water is let out of the tanks. This makes the submarine come up to the surface again.

Some submarines are used for underwater exploration. Scientists use them to find out about sea creatures, or about the sea bed itself.

Sundial

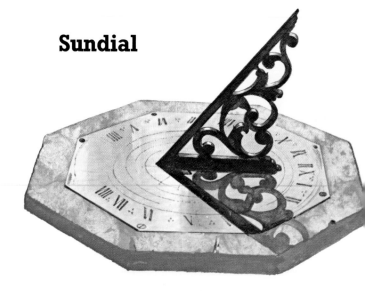

The top of a sundial is marked like a clock. When the sun shines, the shadow of the pointer points to the correct time. The Earth slowly turns round each day. As it turns, the shadow of the pointer moves to show the time.

Below: A submarine on the surface. Its long thin body gives it great speed underwater.

Supertanker

Supertankers are the biggest ships in the world. They carry huge loads of oil. The whole ship is really a large fuel tank.

The crew live at one end of the ship. Sometimes they use bicycles to get from one part of the deck to another. It can take 20 minutes to walk from the bow to the stern of the largest tankers. Tankers have to travel very slowly because they are so large.

When the tanker reaches a port, the oil is taken off in pipes. It is stored on shore until it is needed.

Swallow

Swallows have long forked tails. They build mud nests on the walls of buildings. They rarely walk on the ground because their legs are short and weak. They swoop and glide in the air. In the autumn, European swallows fly all the way to the warmth of South Africa. They stay there during the winter. Then they fly back. American swallows fly to South America and spend the winter there.

Synagogue

Synagogues are buildings where Jewish people pray to God. One side is built facing the holy city of Jerusalem. There are synagogues all over the world. The Jewish holy day is Saturday. The Jewish people go to synagogues on that day. Their holy book, the Torah, is the first five books of the Bible.

T Taj Mahal Tea Telephone

Taj Mahal

The Taj Mahal is one of the most famous and beautiful buildings in the world. It is in India. It was built by an Indian emperor who lived about 350 years ago. He built it as a tomb for his wife. The Taj Mahal is made of white marble. It is richly decorated and took many years to build.

Tea

Tea is a popular drink in many countries. It is made by pouring hot water on to leaves from the tea plant. Tea plants are grown in warm wet countries. Many tea plants grow in India, Sri Lanka and China. This man is picking leaves from a tea bush. The leaves are later dried and roasted.

Telephone

Telephones allow us to speak to people far away. When you phone someone up, you dial or press the number of their telephone. Then you speak into the mouthpiece. Your voice travels along wires to the other person's telephone. Some telephones have no wires. They work by radio waves. You can carry them with you or use them in a car.

Television

Television pictures are sent through the air on radio waves. You cannot see or hear these waves. Television aerials pick up the waves. Television sets turn them into sound and pictures. Satellites are used to send television pictures over great distances, even from one side of the world to the other.

Theatre

Plays, ballets and operas are performed in theatres. In the theatre there is a stage. This is where the actors, singers or dancers perform. The audience sits in long rows facing or around the stage. Their seats are built on a slope so that everyone can see the stage. Painted scenery makes the stage look like the scene in the play.

The performers wait behind the stage until it is time for them to appear. They get ready in small rooms called dressing-rooms.

Below: A theatre in London.

Thermometer

Thermometers measure how hot or cold things are. They are made of glass tubes filled with mercury or alcohol. Some measure the temperature of our bodies. The warmer we are the higher the mercury moves up the tube. Other thermometers measure the temperature of the air. They are used by people like weather forecasters.

Tiger

Tigers are large striped members of the cat family. They live in India and other parts of Asia. Today tigers are becoming quite rare.

Tigers do not mind cold weather. Some live in snowy mountain areas. In hot weather tigers swim in rivers to keep cool. Most cats do not swim, but tigers swim well. Baby tigers are called cubs.

All tigers are meat-eaters. Their stripes help them hide in long grass. They wait there for their prey and leap out to catch an animal to eat.

Tortoise

Tortoises are reptiles that have lived on Earth for 200 million years. They have changed very little in all that time. They are covered in a hard bony shell and they move very slowly. When a tortoise is in danger it pulls its head back into its shell for protection. All tortoises are plant-eaters. Baby tortoises hatch out of eggs.

Trawler

Trawlers are fishing boats. They carry large nets. The net opens out under the water. Fish swim into the net as it drags along behind the boat. Then they are pulled aboard the trawler. Trawlers are strong boats. They can sail in rough seas.

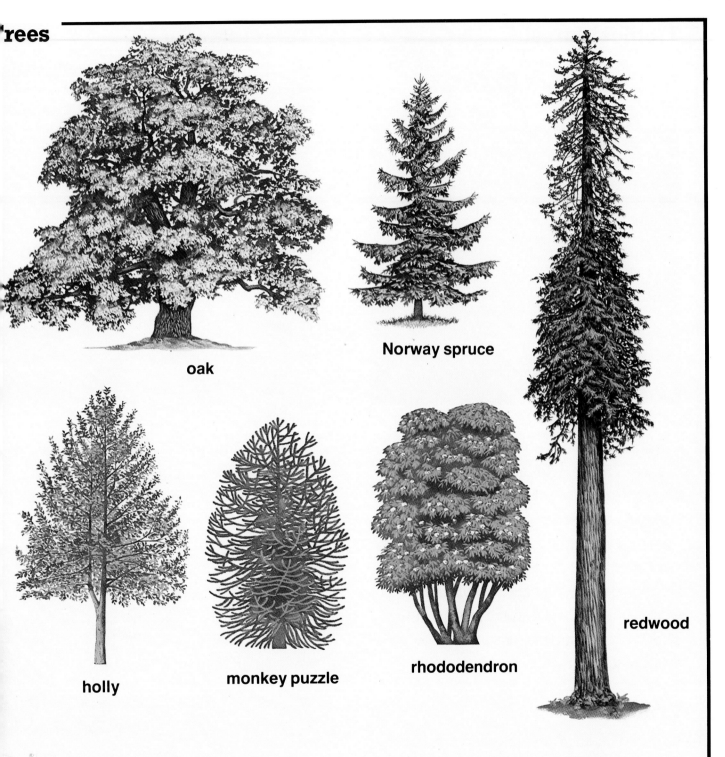

oak

Norway spruce

holly

monkey puzzle

rhododendron

redwood

Trees are very large plants. They have thick, woody stems called trunks. Narrow tubes inside the trunk carry water up from the roots to the leaves. Each year the trunk gets thicker. Many trees are cut down. Their trunks are made into timber and paper.

Some trees, like the oak, lose their leaves in autumn. Some, like the holly, keep their leaves all year. The Redwood is the largest tree in the world. It grows up to 100 metres tall.

Tropical forest

Tropical forests are very hot damp places. They are found near the Equator. There are huge tropical forests in South America and Africa. Rain falls there every day. All the plants and trees grow very quickly and block out the sunlight. Huge creeping plants grow up the trees. Many animals live in the trees. Thousands of insects live on the floor of the forests.

Truck

A truck is a large vehicle that can carry heavy loads. These are dump trucks. They have big wide tyres and powerful engines. Stones from this quarry are loaded on to the trucks. Then the trucks take the stones away. The backs of the trucks can tip up to empty out all the stones in a different place.

Tutankhamun

Tutankhamun was a pharaoh, or ruler, of Egypt. He lived about 3000 years ago and died when he was about 19 years old.

For thousands of years his tomb lay hidden in the sand in Egypt. Then, in 1922, archaeologists discovered it. They found his body inside the tomb in a golden coffin. The wall-painting above is from Tutankhamun's tomb.

USA

About 215 million people live in the United States of America (USA). It is one of the richest and most powerful countries in the world. It is also a very large country. In the north, frozen snow covers the ground. In the south, there are hot, dry deserts. The capital city of the USA is Washington. Many of the big cities, such as New York, are on or near the east coast.

The USA is rich in oil, coal and gas. It produces most of the world's cars and planes. Huge amounts of timber, cotton, tobacco and wheat are grown there.

USSR

The Union of Soviet Socialist Republics (USSR) is the largest country in the world. It is a powerful country and is very rich. About 257 million people live there. The capital city of the USSR is Moscow.

The north of the USSR is in the Arctic. In parts of the south there are hot deserts. Much of the land is a vast flat plain. Wheat and other cereals grow there. There are many mines, oilfields, factories and large farms in the USSR.

V Vegetables Volcano

Vegetables

Vegetables are parts of plants. They make good food and help to keep us healthy. We eat different parts of plants. We eat roots, stems, leaves, flowers, seeds and fruit.

Carrots and radishes are roots. Celery and asparagus are stems. Potatoes and onions are swollen parts of stems that live underground. Cabbages and lettuces are plant leaves. Cauliflowers are flowers that we eat. Peas and beans are seeds.

Some things that we call vegetables are really fruits. Fruit contains seeds, so tomatoes and marrows are fruits.

Volcano

A volcano is a mountain with a hole in its centre. This hole goes deep into the Earth. It reaches the red-hot liquid rock inside the Earth. This rock is called lava. When a volcano erupts, lava and pieces of rock and ash shoot out of the top.

The red-hot lava runs down the sides of the mountain. When it cools it goes hard. Every time this happens the volcano gets larger. The lava builds up the volcano's smooth shape. Many of the volcanoes in the world do not erupt any more.

Washington (1732-1799)

George Washington was a very famous American. He led the American armies to victory against the British. He was made the first President of the United States. The capital city of the USA is named after him. It is called Washington.

Water

Nothing on Earth can live without water. More than half of your body is made up of water. There is a lot of water in the food we eat. Sea water and river water cover much of the Earth.

Water is brought to our homes in pipes. This water has been cleaned to make sure there are no germs in it to make us ill. We use water for drinking, washing and cooking.

The water we drink is a liquid. When it is heated it turns to steam. When it is frozen it turns into ice.

Waterfall

Waterfalls are found where there is a steep drop in a river bed. The water plunges over the rocky edge and falls to a lower level. Some waterfalls are huge. The power of the falling water can be used to turn engines to make electricity. This waterfall is in South America. It is twice as tall as the highest building in the world.

W Weather

Weather

Rain

Fog

Snow

Hail

Sun

Cloud

Rainbow

Wind

Thunder

Whale

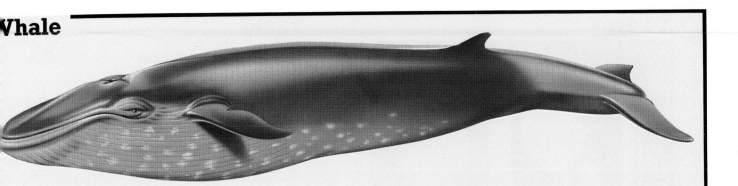

Whales are large mammals that live in the sea. They use lungs for breathing and they come up to the surface to breathe. Baby whales are born alive into the sea and they feed on their mothers' milk. Some whales eat tiny sea creatures. Others eat large fish.

This is a blue whale. It is the largest animal in the world. Some blue whales can weigh as much as 30 elephants. Whales are becoming rare because they are hunted for their oil and meat.

Wood

Wood comes from the trunks and branches of trees. When the trees are cut down the wood is sawn up into pieces. The pieces are then dried. They can be made into many useful things. Wood is used to make tiny matchsticks. It is also used to make the framework of some buildings and boats. We use it to make furniture. Paper is made from wood. Wood can also be burned to make a very useful fuel.

Wool

Most wool is made from the thick curly hair of sheep. Once a year, the sheep's woolly coat is cut off. Then it can be spun into long threads and dyed different colours. Some wool is made into balls of yarn for knitting. Some is woven into woollen cloth.

Clothes made from wool are very warm. The hair of camels and some goats and rabbits can be made into wool in the same way.

XYZ X-rays Xylophone Yacht
Zebra

X-rays

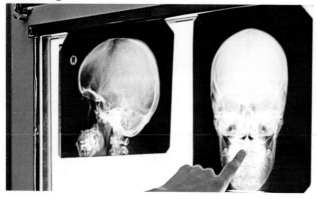

Doctors and dentists use X-rays to study the inside of our bodies. The X-rays pass through the body and photograph the inside. The doctor can see if something is wrong. Today scanners can build up a picture of the whole body.

Xylophone

Xylophones are musical instruments. This is the kind of xylophone used in an orchestra. It is on a stand with four legs. On top there are wooden bars. Each is a different size. They are struck with sticks to make different musical notes.

Yacht

Yachts are boats used for pleasure or sport. Many yachts have engines as well as sails. Very fast yachts are used for racing across the oceans. These have tall triangular sails. People have sailed all round the world in yachts.

Zebra

Zebras live in Africa. They are striped animals that look like horses. Zebras live together in groups and eat grass. Each one has its own pattern of stripes. The stripes help it hide in the long grass. The lion is a zebra's most dangerous enemy.

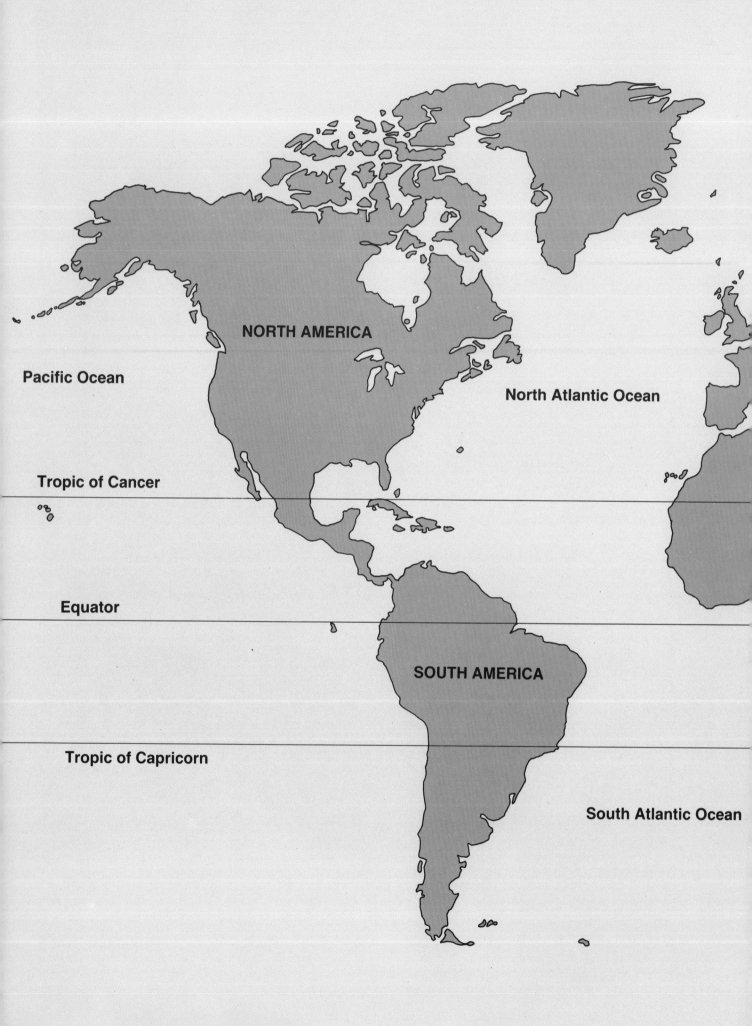